LOSING WEIGHT THE Smart WAY

SmartPoints™

LOSING WEIGHT THE Smart WAY

DELICIOUS RECIPES FOR A HEALTHIER, HAPPIER LIFE

weightwatchers

SIMON &
SCHUSTER

London · New York · Sydney · Toronto · New Delhi

A CBS COMPANY

THE SMALL PRINT

EGGS We use medium eggs, unless otherwise stated. Pregnant women, the elderly and children should avoid recipes with eggs which are not fully cooked or raw.

FRUIT AND VEGETABLES Our recipes use medium-sized fruit and veg, unless otherwise stated.

REDUCED FAT SOFT CHEESE Where a recipe uses reduced fat soft cheese, we mean a soft cheese with 25% less fat than its full fat equivalent.

LOW FAT SPREAD When a recipe uses a low fat spread, we mean a spread with a fat content of no less than 38%.

MICROWAVES If we have used a microwave in any of our recipes, the timings will be for an 850 watt microwave oven.

PREP AND COOKING TIMES These are approximate and meant to be guidelines. Prep time includes all the steps up to and following the main cooking time(s). Cooking times may vary according to your oven. Before serving chicken, always check that there is no pink meat and that the juices run clear by piercing with a sharp knife or skewer.

The use of the term 'gluten free' or the 'gluten free icon' is illustrative only. Weight Watchers is not responsible for the presence of gluten in the dishes that have not been prepared in accordance with instructions; nor is it responsible for gluten contamination due to an external cause. Recipes labelled as gluten free, or displaying the gluten free icon, only include ingredients that naturally do not contain gluten. Whenever using canned, bottled or other types of packaged processed ingredients, such as sauces and stocks, it is essential to check that those ingredients do not contain gluten.

Disclaimer: The exercises suggested are intended for healthy adult individuals and are not intended for use by minors, or individuals with any type of health condition. Weight Watchers strongly advises you to consult your doctor if you have concerns about your health before you undertake any of the exercises described. Weight Watchers and the Publisher will not be held responsible for and are released from any liability in respect of any injuries or other problems that may result from your participation in the exercises.

First published in Great Britain by Simon & Schuster UK Ltd, 2016
A CBS Company

Copyright © 2016, Weight Watchers International, Inc.

Simon & Schuster UK Ltd
222 Gray's Inn Road
London WC1X 8HB
www.simonandschuster.co.uk
Simon & Schuster Australia, Sydney
Simon & Schuster India, New Delhi

This book is copyright under the Berne Convention.
No reproduction without permission.
All rights reserved.

10 9 8 7 6 5 4 3 2 1

Weight Watchers, **SmartPoints** and the **SmartPoints** icon are the registered trademarks of Weight Watchers International Inc. and used under license by Weight Watchers (UK) Ltd. All rights reserved.

Weight Watchers Publications Team:
Imogen Prescott, Samantha Rees, Stephanie Williams
Photography: William Shaw
Recipe development and food preparation: Penny Stephens
Prop styling: Sarah Waller

For Simon & Schuster:
Senior Commissioning Editor: Nicky Hill
Design: Corinna Farrow
Production Manager: Katherine Thornton

Colour Reproduction by Aylesbury Studios Ltd, UK
Printed and bound in Germany

A CIP catalogue record for this book is available from the British Library

ISBN: 978-1-47115-386-0

Pictured on front cover, clockwise from top left: Raw beetroot; Three cheese cannelloni, p.124; Pork and apricot burgers with sweet potato chips, p.176; Chilli, carrot and spinach soup, p.154; Courgette spaghetti, p.174; African vegetable stew with sweet potatoes and peanuts p.126
Back cover, left to right: Classic lasagne, p.96; Easy smoked salmon tortilla with salsa, p.38; Raw brownies, p.214

contents

WELCOME TO
losing weight the smart way —

THE COOKBOOK THAT WILL NOURISH YOU INSIDE AND OUT.

We love food. It's one of life's greatest joys. It nourishes us and keeps us strong. We don't believe in ever going hungry and we don't believe any food should be forbidden. We also believe that eating healthier makes life better; food should taste delicious and make us feel amazing.

SmartPoints reflects the latest in nutritional science. Instead of focusing on calories (which don't tell the whole story) **SmartPoints** will nudge you towards nutritious foods that are lower in sugar and saturated fat, and higher in protein. With two ways to follow the plan – Count and No Count – you can switch between them whenever you want and lose weight, all while eating delicious food. It's all about finding out what works best for you today.

In this book we have given you lots of ideas to create some seriously good food in your kitchen. There are easy recipes for breakfast (or brunch, or lunch…), ideas for pulling together something quickly and, of course, lots of favourites. If you fancy dipping your toe in the world of chia seeds and freekeh, we've come up with some really good 'clean living'-style recipes that use ingredients you may not have come across before. And we've rebelled against the notion that a salad should consist of a few limp lettuce leaves and a couple of cherry tomatoes with our 'Let's start a salad revolution' chapter – loads of delicious ideas that prove salad doesn't have to be boring! And we know that your success goes beyond just the number on the scales; it's a combination of how you feel, your confidence, health and happiness (and so much more). That's why we've included some handy tips in here that will get you moving as well as make you think a bit more about yourself. And, as usual, this book is really easy to use – check out the symbols below, which will help in making the best decision about what to eat, for you.

SIGN LANGUAGE

0 The number inside the **SmartPoints** coin tells you how many **SmartPoints** are in the recipe.

● A No Count recipe. You can make this recipe and eat the lot knowing you don't have to count it.

GF A recipe that is totally gluten free or can be made gluten free with a few simple swaps. So if we say soy sauce, make sure you use a gluten free version.

V Vegetarian.

YOUR HANDY
no count FOODS LIST

IF YOU'VE CHOSEN TO FOLLOW THE NO COUNT APPROACH THEN FOCUS YOUR EATING ON THIS LIST OF HEALTHY FOODS. ANY RECIPES IN THIS BOOK THAT ARE SUITABLE FOR WHEN YOU'RE NOT COUNTING HAVE THE ◉ SYMBOL BESIDE THEM.

Bacon medallions
Baked beans

Beans & pulses
Aduki
Black eyed
Borlotti
Broad
Butter
Cannellini
Chick peas
Flageolet
French
Green
Haricot
Kidney
Lentils
Mixed pulses
Mung
Pinto
Runner
Soya
Split peas

Beef
Braising steak, lean
Fillet steak, lean
Mince, extra lean (5% fat)
Rump steak, lean
Silverside, lean
Sirloin steak, lean
Stewing steak, lean

Bread, brown, calorie controlled

Buckwheat
Bulgur wheat

Cheese
Cottage cheese, reduced fat, natural
Quark

Chicken
Breast, skinless
Drumstick, skinless
Leg, skinless
Mince
Wafer thin

Couscous, wholewheat
Crumpets

Eggs
Duck
Egg white
Goose
Hen
Quail

Fish*
Cod, fresh or smoked
Coley
Dover Sole
Grouper
Haddock, fresh or smoked
Hake
Halibut
Herring roe, soft
Hoki

John Dory
Lemon sole
Monkfish
Mullet
Orange roughy
Pike
Plaice
Pollock
Red snapper
Rock salmon
Salmon
Salmon, tinned, pink/red
Sardines
Sea bass
Sea bream (Red Fish)
Shark
Skate
Squid
Swordfish
Tilapia
Trout
Trout, smoked
Tuna
Tuna in brine/spring water
Turbot
Whiting

Fromage frais, natural
Fromage frais, natural, fat free

Fruit
Canned in natural juice, drained
Fresh (except avocado)
Frozen

Gammon steak, lean
Garlic
Ginger
Goat
Guinea fowl

Ham
Premium
Pre-packed slices
Wafer thin

Heart, lamb's
Herbs, fresh

Jelly, sugar free

Kidney
Lamb
Pig

Liver
Calf
Chicken
Lamb
Ox
Pig

Meat free
Bacon style rashers
Fillets
Mince
Pieces
Soya mince
Tofu, regular/smoked

Milk
Skimmed
Unsweetened almond
Unsweetened soya

Millet

Nori

Oat Bran
Oats

Octopus

Partridge
Passata
Pasta, wholewheat
Pigeon
Popping corn kernels

Pork
Escalope
Fillet, lean
Leg, lean
Loin steak, lean
Mince, extra lean (5% fat)
Shoulder, lean
Tenderloin

Potatoes, all types

Puffed wheat, no added sugar or salt

Quail
Quinoa

Rabbit

Rice
Brown
Wild

Sandwich thins, brown
Seafood sticks

Shellfish
Clams
Cockles
Crab
Crab in brine, drained
Crayfish
Lobster
Mussels
Oysters
Prawns, all types
Scallops
Shrimps
Whelks

Winkles

Turkey
Breast, mince
Breast, skinless
Roasted, skinless
Steak
Thigh, skinless
Wafer thin

Veal escalope

Vegetables:
Canned in water
Fresh
Frozen

Venison, lean

Wheat bran
Wheat germ
Wholegrain wheat cereal (similar to
     Shredded Wheat)

Yam

Yogurt
Greek, 0% fat, natural
Fat free, natural
Low fat, natural
Soya, plain

Weight Watchers Products
Extra Trimmed Unsmoked Back
     Bacon
Greek Style Natural Yogurt
Original Breakfast Oats
Petits Pains
Pitta Bread; White and Wholemeal
Quark
Sliced Brown Danish Bread
Tortillas
Wraps

* Check www.goodfishguide.co.uk/
pocket-goodfishguide

A GUIDE TO seasonal FOODS

Summer

Apples . Apricots . Blackcurrants . Blueberries .
Cherries . Damsons . Figs . Gooseberries . Grapes .
Greengages . Melons . Nectarines . Peaches .
Plums . Raspberries . Redcurrants .
Strawberries . Asparagus . Aubergines . Beetroot .
Broad beans . Carrots . Chard . Chicory . Chillies .
Courgettes . Cucumber . Fennel .
French beans . Globe artichokes . Herbs .
Kohlrabi . Mangetout . Marrows . New potatoes .
Peas . Peppers . Potatoes . Radishes . Rocket .
Runner beans . Salad leaves . Spring onions .
Sweetcorn . Tomatoes . Watercress .
Crab . Grey mullet . Mackerel . Salmon .
Sardines . Scallops . Sea bass .
English veal . Grouse . Lamb . Venison .

Spring

Alphonso mangoes . Apricots . Blood oranges .
Gooseberries . Nectarines . Rhubarb .
Asparagus . Cabbages . Carrots .
Chicory . Globe artichokes . Herbs .
Jersey Royals . Leeks . Morels .
New potatoes . Parsnips . Purple
sprouting broccoli . Radishes . Rocket .
Salad leaves . Shallots . Spinach .
Spring onions . Watercress . Crab .
Herrings . Lemon sole . Mackerel .
Mussels . Oysters .
Salmon . Sardines . Scallops .
Sea bass . Sea trout .
Wild salmon . Guinea fowl .
Spring lamb . Venison .

For the best flavours, as well as real value for money, try to eat fruit, vegetables, fish and meat according to what's in season. Check out our food 'rainbow' for lots of inspiration throughout the seasons.

Autumn

· Apples · Blackberries · Chestnuts · Clementines · · Cranberries · Damsons · Dates · Figs · Greengages · · Melons · Nectarines · Pears · Plums · · Pomegranates · Quince · Satsumas · Sloes · · Walnuts ● Aubergines · Broccoli · Brussels sprouts · · Butternut squash · Cabbages · Carrots · Cauliflower · · Celeriac · Celery · Chard · Chillies · Fennel · · French beans · Herbs · Jerusalem artichokes · · Kale · Marrows · Mushrooms · Parsnips · Peppers · · Potatoes · Pumpkins · Runner beans · Salad leaves · · Spring onions · Swede · Sweetcorn · Tomatoes · · Truffles · Wild mushrooms ● Clams · · Grey mullet · Mackerel · Mussels · · Oysters · Scallops · Sea bass · · Game birds · Lamb · Venison ·

Winter

· Blood oranges · Chestnuts · Clementines · · Cranberries · Dates · Forced rhubarb · · Oranges · Pomegranates · Satsumas · · Seville oranges ● Brussels sprouts · · Cabbages · Celeriac · Celery · Cauliflower · Chicory · · Jerusalem artichokes · Kale · · Leeks · Parsnips · Purple · · Sprouting broccoli · Swede · · Truffles · Turnips ● Clams · · Herrings · John Dory · · Mackerel · Mussels · Oysters · · Scallops · Sea bass · · Goose · Guinea fowl · · Turkey · Venison ·

YOUR TOP 10
pantry essentials

Eating healthy, delicious food shouldn't be hard work. We think good food should be easy to prepare, so check out our recommendations for kitchen essentials to make it even easier.

YOU SAY TOMAYTO. I SAY TOMAHTO. We know you know, but we thought it might be worth reminding you how superbly versatile canned tomatoes are. If you're ever stuck for what to cook, grab a can of tomatoes out of the cupboard (chopped, plum, cherry, passata) or some fresh ones out of the fridge and, hey presto, you have the base for pasta sauce, curry, casserole, bolognese, chilli, tagine… the list goes on.

SPICE OF LIFE. Dried spices can transform any dish – grow your collection over time and you'll never run out of ideas.

HERBTASTIC. Dried are perfect for adding to dishes that have enough cooking time to let them infuse, and fresh can add real flavour to quick-cook dishes, coming into their own when they're added just at the end of the cooking time. Check out fresh herbs in salads – mint and coriander can add a real zing to a plain lettuce leaf salad.

PASTA DOES IT. Top of the list for a pantry essential – no kitchen should be without pasta. And wholewheat pasta is perfect if you're on a No Count day.

RICE IS NICE. Whether it's brown rice, long grain rice, white rice, wild rice or basmati rice – keep a packet in your cupboard. Brown and wild are also super-helpful to have if you're on a No Count day.

G.A.R.L.I.C. Lazy or fresh, it's always good to have some garlic knocking about in your kitchen – it gives a real home-made flavour to cooking, and can be used in so many dishes.

PASS THE TISSUES. How many times have we planned meals in our heads then gone to start cooking to find – catastrophe! – no onions? Onions are so versatile and form the basis of many meals. Make sure you always have them in stock.

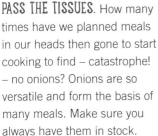

STOCK UP. Tiny little flavour capsules that can give oomph to whatever you're prepping in the kitchen. Try to choose stock cubes or pots that are low in salt, and remember that some brands now offer gluten free options.

YOUR EGGCELLENCY. We just couldn't leave the trusty egg off our essentials list; used in sweet and savoury dishes, as a base, or simply perfect on their own.

OIL LOVE IT. Experiment with different oils to find the ones you like the most; there are a huge number available. Olive oil is a must for salads, and if you buy an oil sprayer you can use all types for cooking without having to worry about the **SmartPoints** values. And for this reason alone, make sure you always have oil in your cupboard ready for cooking.

quick SmartPoints VALUES INDEX

0 SmartPoints value
Veg & bamboo shoot clear soup **148** (0) GF V

0 SmartPoints value
Tropical fruit salad **208** (0) GF V

0 SmartPoints value
Vegetable stock **220** (0) GF V

1 SmartPoints value
Chilli, carrot & spinach soup **154** GF V

1 SmartPoints value
Cevice **172** (0) GF

1 SmartPoints value
Summer berry spread **206** GF V

1 SmartPoints value
Harissa **216** (0) GF V

1 SmartPoints value
Tomato ketchup **218** GF V

2 SmartPoints value
Home-made lemonade with mint **134** GF V

2 SmartPoints value
Hearty lentil & vegetable soup **144** GF V

2 SmartPoints value
Butternut & coriander soup **150** GF V

2 SmartPoints value
Nutty butters **204** GF V

3 SmartPoints value
Thai beef lettuce cups **64** GF

3 SmartPoints value
A really pretty courgette & mint salad **78** (0) V

3 SmartPoints value
Watercress & roasted garlic soup **140** (0) GF V

3 SmartPoints value
Speedy garlic, chilli & coriander prawns **170** (0) GF

3 SmartPoints value
Romesco **216** GF V

4 SmartPoints value
Balsamic leek & goat's cheese tarts **42** V

4 SmartPoints value
Chicken & spring vegetable stew **112**

4 SmartPoints value
Really fresh spiced celery juice **134** GF V

4 SmartPoints value
Super-smooth celeriac & fennel soup **142** GF V

5 SmartPoints value
Beef pho **162** GF

5 SmartPoints value
Bacon & roasted tomato crumpets **24** (0)

5 SmartPoints value
Potato farls & poached egg **30** GF V

5 SmartPoints value
Spicy barbecued fish wraps **44**

5 SmartPoints value
Thai chicken salad **56**

5 SmartPoints value
Simple steak & roast butternut salad **62** O GF

5 SmartPoints value
Sweet potato & turkey chilli **114** O GF

5 SmartPoints value
Blueberry soy smoothie **132** GF V

5 SmartPoints value
Creamy coconut & avocado **136** GF V

5 SmartPoints value
Sweetcorn, chilli & coriander soup **156** O GF V

5 SmartPoints value
Classic pea & ham soup **164** O GF

5 SmartPoints value
Nachos with black bean salsa **188** V

5 SmartPoints value
Orange freekeh chicken **200** O

6 SmartPoints value
Porridge with caramelised bananas & blueberries **20** V

6 SmartPoints value
Granola with raspberries **28** GF V

6 SmartPoints value
Must-try broad bean bruschetta **46** V

6 SmartPoints value
Spiced duck & grapefruit salad **54** GF

6 SmartPoints value
Chicken Caesar with pear & walnuts **58**

6 SmartPoints value
Super-easy panzanella **76** V

6 SmartPoints value
Lentil salad with goat's cheese & roast peppers **84** GF V

6 SmartPoints value
Pork & rosemary stuffed peppers **100**

6 SmartPoints value
Simple Tuscan fish stew **118**

6 SmartPoints value
Mini lentil pies **122** V

6 SmartPoints value
Mango & pistachio lassi **132** GF V

6 SmartPoints value
Rhubarb & pear with ginger & honey **136** GF V

6 SmartPoints value
Spinach & potato soup with pesto & egg **152** GF V

6 SmartPoints value
Spring minestrone **160**

7 SmartPoints value

Scrambled egg with spinach on rye 22 Ⓥ

7 SmartPoints value

Sticky sausage open sarnie 26

7 SmartPoints value

Thai fishcakes with fresh cucumber salad 36 Ⓞ GF

7 SmartPoints value

Easy smoked salmon tortilla with salsa 38

7 SmartPoints value

Farfalle with prawns, watercress & capers 68

7 SmartPoints value

Simply lovely rice paper prawn rolls 70 GF

7 SmartPoints value

Sesame & lime tuna salad 72 GF

7 SmartPoints value

Lamb meatballs & aubergine in tomato sauce 88 GF

7 SmartPoints value

Beautiful salmon with beetroot rösti & cucumber sauce 116

7 SmartPoints value

Fish finger wraps 120

7 SmartPoints value

Curried parsnip soup 138 GF Ⓥ

7 SmartPoints value

Spicy sweet potato & coconut soup 146 GF Ⓥ

7 SmartPoints value

Hearty golden vegetable soup 158 Ⓞ GF Ⓥ

7 SmartPoints value

Tomato & prawn courgette spaghetti 174

7 SmartPoints value

Lemon & thyme pork escalopes with chargrilled veg 178

7 SmartPoints value

Raw brownies 214 GF Ⓥ

8 SmartPoints value

Griddled chicken salad with asparagus & Parmesan 60 GF Ⓥ

8 SmartPoints value

Sweet potato, bulgur wheat & prosciutto salad 66

8 SmartPoints value

Classic chicken cordon bleu 106

8 SmartPoints value

Socca with peppers, tomatoes & avocado 196 GF Ⓥ

8 SmartPoints value

Zesty trout with warm broad & butter beans 202 GF

8 SmartPoints value

Buckwheat pancakes with coconut yogurt 210 GF Ⓥ

8 SmartPoints value

Chia seed snack bars 212 GF Ⓥ

9 SmartPoints value

Chicken sandwich with a herby lemon mayo 40

9 SmartPoints value

Quick feta & watermelon salad 80 GF Ⓥ

9 SmartPoints value

Really easy asparagus with griddled halloumi **82** GF V

9 SmartPoints value

Roast chicken with fat oven chips **108** GF

9 SmartPoints value

Chicken, leek & cider pie **110**

9 SmartPoints value

Three cheese cannelloni **124** V

9 SmartPoints value

African veg stew with sweet potatoes & peanuts **126** GF V

10 SmartPoints value

Cannellini beans & chorizo on toast **32**

10 SmartPoints value

Steak & pesto pitta **34**

10 SmartPoints value

Goat's cheese, Parma ham & strawberry salad **74**

10 SmartPoints value

Beef ragù with tagliatelle **90**

10 SmartPoints value

Seared steak with salsa verde **94** No Count GF

10 SmartPoints value

Ultimate gammon & egg pie **98**

11 SmartPoints value

Coconut & ginger beef curry **92**

11 SmartPoints value

Classic lasagne **96**

11 SmartPoints value

Best ever toad in the hole with mustard gravy **102**

11 SmartPoints value

Plaice with peas, lettuce & pancetta **168** GF

11 SmartPoints value

Ham & petits pois pasta **180**

11 SmartPoints value

Mixed pepper & sausage pizza **182**

11 SmartPoints value

Orzo risotto with water-cress, blue cheese & walnuts **186** V

11 SmartPoints value

Beetroot quinoa risotto with goat's cheese **194** GF V

11 SmartPoints value

Warm beetroot, baby kale & halloumi salad **198** GF V

12 SmartPoints value

Blue cheese gnocchi gratin **184** V

13 SmartPoints value

Chipotle pork with chimichurri & slaw **104** GF

14 SmartPoints value

Pork & apricot burgers with sweet potato chips **176**

No Count
 GF Gluten Free
 V Vegetarian

breakfast, brunch, lunch?

porridge WITH CARAMELISED BANANAS AND BLUEBERRIES

6 SmartPoints value

SmartPoints values per serving 6
SmartPoints values per recipe 24

V

Takes 5 minutes
Serves 4

125 g porridge oats
500 ml skimmed milk
1 teaspoon agave nectar, or according
   to taste
calorie controlled cooking spray
1 banana, sliced
1 tablespoon honey
150 g blueberries

A breakfast that's bursting with goodness. It's so quick and easy to make, too.

1. Mix together the oats, milk and agave nectar in a microwavable bowl and cook on full power for 2 minutes.

2. Meanwhile, heat a non-stick frying pan and mist with the cooking spray. Add the banana and cook over a medium heat for 1–2 minutes until lightly caramelised. Drizzle over the honey and add the blueberries. Shake the pan and let it bubble for 1 minute. Spoon over the hot porridge and serve.

FIND OUT MORE ABOUT THE POWER OF BLUEBERRIES ON PAGE 190.

scrambled egg
WITH SPINACH ON RYE

SmartPoints values per serving 7
SmartPoints values per recipe 13

Takes 10 minutes
Serves 2

calorie controlled cooking spray
6 spring onions, sliced finely
2 eggs, beaten
3 tablespoons skimmed milk
2 x 60 g slices dark rye bread
150 g baby leaf spinach
salt and freshly ground black pepper
Tabasco sauce

Flavourful and nourishing, this dish makes a satisfying veggie brunch or light lunch.

1. Mist a non-stick frying pan with the cooking spray, add the spring onions and cook for 2 minutes until softened. Add the eggs and milk, season well and cook gently, stirring often, until lightly set.

2. Meanwhile, toast the rye bread and cook the spinach in a large pan with a splash of water until just wilted. Drain and season. Halve the rye toast, divide between 2 plates and top with the spinach and scrambled egg. Serve with a good splash of Tabasco sauce.

○ To make this a No Count option, use 2 slices brown calorie controlled bread instead for 4 **SmartPoints** values.

GF To make this a gluten free option, swap the dark rye bread for 2 x 35 g slices gluten free brown bread for 6 **SmartPoints** values.

BACON AND ROASTED TOMATO
crumpets

SmartPoints values per serving 5
SmartPoints values per recipe 19

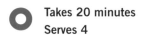

Takes 20 minutes
Serves 4

8 lean smoked bacon medallions
250 g cherry tomatoes
½ teaspoon olive oil
a pinch of sea salt
a handful of basil leaves
4 crumpets

If you're a fan of cooked breakfasts, this bacon and roasted tomato combo will hit the spot.

1. Preheat the oven to Gas Mark 5/190°C/fan oven 170°C. Sandwich the bacon medallions between two baking sheets to keep them flat and cook on the top shelf of the oven for 15 minutes.

2. Meanwhile, put the tomatoes on a baking tray, drizzle with the olive oil and sprinkle with the sea salt. When the bacon medallions have been cooking for 5 minutes, put the tomatoes and a few of the basil leaves in the oven for 10 minutes to roast. Toast the crumpets.

3. Drain the bacon medallions on kitchen paper, tear in pieces and roughly crush the tomatoes. Serve the toasted crumpets with the tomatoes and bacon pieces on top, garnished with the rest of the basil leaves.

sticky sausage
OPEN SARNIE

7 SmartPoints per serving 7
SmartPoints values per recipe 14

Takes 35 minutes
Serves 2

3 reduced fat sausages
1 red onion, cut into thin wedges
1 teaspoon olive oil
2 tablespoons redcurrant jelly
a pinch of chilli flakes (optional)
a handful of rocket
2 x 25 g slices wholemeal bread

Who can resist a sausage sandwich? Try this delicious sticky version for a lazy brunch or lunch for two.

1. Preheat the oven to Gas Mark 6/200°C/fan oven 180°C. Place the sausages and onion wedges in a small roasting tin, drizzle with the olive oil and bake for 25 minutes, turning occasionally, until golden brown and cooked through.

2. Dot the sausages and onions with the redcurrant jelly and sprinkle with the chilli flakes if using. Bake for another 5 minutes until sticky.

3. Chop the sausages up into chunky pieces. Divide the sausages, onions and rocket between the 2 slices of bread. Serve immediately.

COOK'S TIP Most reduced fat sausages come in packets of 8, so freeze the remaining 5, either raw or cooked and cooled, and keep for another day.

granola
WITH RASPBERRIES

 6 SmartPoints value™

SmartPoints values per serving 6
SmartPoints values per recipe 38

 GF
V

Preparation time 10 minutes
Cooking time 25–30 minutes
        + cooling
Serves 6

120 g gluten free porridge oats
1 tablespoon sesame seeds
25 g flaked almonds
½ teaspoon ground cinnamon
1 egg white
2 tablespoons clear honey
a few drops of almond extract (optional)
25 g dried apple, chopped
600 g 0% fat natural Greek yogurt,
    to serve
250 g raspberries, to serve

A really rather luxurious breakfast with creamy yogurt and juicy berries – a great way to start the day.

1. Heat the oven to Gas Mark 2/150°C/fan oven 130°C. Line a large baking sheet with non-stick baking paper. In a large bowl, mix together the oats, sesame seeds, almonds and cinnamon. In a small bowl, whisk the egg white until frothy, add the honey and almond extract (if using) and whisk again. Add to the oat mixture and mix well. Stir in the apple and scatter the mixture on to the baking tray.

2. Bake for 25–30 minutes, or until golden, stirring once. Allow to cool on the tray. Serve with the yogurt and a handful of raspberries.

VARIATION If you use 100 ml skimmed milk per person instead of the yogurt, the **SmartPoints** values per serving will be the same. On its own, the granola has a **SmartPoints** value of 4 per serving.

> **🍴 COOK'S TIP** You can store the cooled granola in an airtight container for up to 3 weeks.

MAKE TIME FOR BREAKFAST –
DON'T RUSH IT. LEARN MORE ON
PAGES 128-9.

POTATO FARLS AND
poached egg

5 SmartPoints value

SmartPoints values per serving 5
SmartPoints values per recipe 20

GF

Takes 25 minutes + cooling
Serves 4

V

450 g peeled baking potatoes
   (about 2 medium potatoes)
30 g gluten free plain flour
a pinch of freshly grated nutmeg
1 teaspoon Dijon mustard
calorie controlled cooking spray
350 g cherry tomatoes, halved
4 very fresh eggs, at room temperature
a few sprigs of fresh parsley, chopped

Potato farls are a Northern Irish speciality. Wonderfully versatile, these triangular-shaped cakes or flatbreads go well with almost anything.

1. Cut the potatoes into 1 cm slices and place them in a saucepan. Cover with water, bring to the boil and cook for 12–14 minutes, or until tender. Drain well and return to the pan. Stir for 1 minute over a low heat to remove any excess moisture. Turn off the heat and crush the potatoes. Leave to cool for 10 minutes and then mash until smooth. Add the flour, nutmeg and mustard and mash again.

2. Line a board with cling film. Shape the potato mixture into a ball and gently press into an 18–20 cm circle on the cling film. Cut into 8. Heat a large non-stick frying pan over a medium heat and mist with the cooking spray. Slide the farls into the pan and cook for 3–4 minutes, or until deep golden. Using a plate or a board, invert the pan and cook the farls on the other side for a further 3–4 minutes.

3. Meanwhile, grill the tomatoes for 5 minutes, or until soft. Bring a large, deep frying pan of water to the boil and carefully crack the eggs into it. Leave for 2–3 minutes to poach at a gentle simmer. Drain and trim any straggly bits.

4. Top the farls with some grilled tomatoes and a soft poached egg. Sprinkle over the parsley and serve.

CANNELLINI *beans* AND *chorizo* ON TOAST

10 SmartPoints value

SmartPoints per serving 10
SmartPoints values per recipe 20

Takes 35 minutes
Serves 2

60 g cooking chorizo, cubed
1 onion, sliced
1 garlic clove, sliced
½ red chilli, chopped
2 tomatoes, de-seeded and chopped
410 g can cannellini beans, drained
1 tablespoon tomato ketchup
2 tablespoons chopped fresh parsley
2 tablespoons chopped fresh coriander
2 slices Weight Watchers malted Danish
    bread
salt and freshly ground black pepper

A traditional standby favourite made over. This delicious version makes a great brunch.

1. Add the chorizo to a hot frying pan and cook until golden and starting to release its oil. Add the onion and cook until soft. Add the garlic and red chilli and cook for a further 1 minute.

2. Tip in the tomatoes and lower the heat. Cook for 2 minutes, then add the beans, ketchup and 100 ml water and continue to cook for 10 minutes, stirring occasionally. Season with salt and pepper, add the herbs and mix well.

3. Toast the bread. Spoon the beans and chorizo over the toast and serve immediately.

GF To make this suitable for a gluten free diet, swap the malted Danish bread for 2 x 35 g slices gluten free brown bread, for 11 **SmartPoints** values.

> **COOK'S TIP** If you have the time, why not try making your own tomato ketchup? Check out our simple ketchup recipe on page 218.

STEAK AND PESTO
pitta

 SmartPoints values per serving 10
SmartPoints values per recipe 10

Takes 20 minutes
Serves 1

10 g pine nuts, toasted
1 garlic clove
a small handful of fresh basil leaves
1 tablespoon lemon juice
2 teaspoons olive oil
5 g Parmesan cheese, grated
calorie controlled cooking spray
60 g lean beef frying steak, sliced
1 Weight Watchers white pitta bread
   (or similar)
1 tomato, sliced
a handful of rocket
salt and freshly ground black pepper

Lean steak in a handy pitta pocket makes a special lunchtime treat for one.

1. To make the pesto, blend the pine nuts and garlic in a food processor. Add the basil leaves, lemon juice and oil and blitz until you have a paste, then mix in the Parmesan cheese. Season the pesto to taste and set aside.

2. Mist a frying pan with the cooking spray and fry the steak for 2 minutes on each side, or until browned and cooked to your liking.

3. Meanwhile, toast the pitta and split it open. Spread the inside of the pitta with half the pesto, covering both sides.

4. Fill the pitta with the tomato, rocket and steak. Top with the remaining pesto and eat while still warm.

GF Swap the white pitta bread for 1 gluten free white pitta bread for 9 **SmartPoints** values.

thai fishcakes WITH FRESH CUCUMBER SALAD

7 SmartPoints values per serving 7
SmartPoints values per recipe 27

 Takes 35 minutes
Serves 4

270 g white fish, such as cod
150 g raw peeled prawns
1 tablespoon Thai fish sauce
4 tablespoons red curry paste
zest of 1 lime
½ bunch of fresh coriander (stalks only;
    retain leaves for the salad)
1 egg white
50 g green beans, sliced thinly
4 teaspoons sunflower oil

For the salad
1 cucumber, de-seeded and sliced
1 red onion, sliced
3 cm fresh root ginger, chopped
fresh coriander leaves (see above)

For the dressing
2 teaspoons rice wine vinegar
1 teaspoon sunflower oil
1 teaspoon sesame oil

These spicy fishcakes with their zingy salad and dressing are incredibly moreish.

1. To make the salad, combine all the ingredients in a bowl. Whisk the dressing ingredients together and pour over the salad. Toss and then set aside while you make the fishcakes.

2. Put all the fishcake ingredients except the beans and oil into a food processor. Pulse until the mixture is smooth. Tip into a bowl, add the green beans and mix together. Form the mixture into 12 fishcakes.

3. Heat half the sunflower oil in a medium frying pan and, when hot, add 6 fishcakes. Cook them for 2–3 minutes on each side and then place them on kitchen paper to absorb the excess oil. Repeat with the remaining fishcakes and sunflower oil. Serve 3 fishcakes per person with the salad on the side.

EASY SMOKED SALMON *tortilla* WITH SALSA

 SmartPoints values per serving 7
SmartPoints values per recipe 27

Takes 10 minutes
Serves 4

4 Weight Watchers tortillas (or similar)
200 g smoked salmon, sliced
100 ml half fat soured cream
lime wedges, to serve
Tabasco sauce, to serve (optional)

For the salsa
4 ripe tomatoes, de-seeded and
　　chopped roughly
¼ cucumber, chopped roughly
1 small red onion, chopped finely
3 tablespoons chopped fresh coriander
juice of ½ lime
salt and freshly ground black pepper

Add a touch of Tex-Mex flair to your lunch with these easy-to-assemble tortillas.

1. To make the salsa, combine all the ingredients in a bowl. Season to taste and set aside.

2. Heat the tortillas according to the packet instructions and place one on each serving plate. Top each with the salsa, some smoked salmon slices and a little soured cream and fold. Serve each with a lime wedge and a drop of Tabasco, if you fancy a spicy kick.

chicken SANDWICH WITH A HERBY LEMON MAYO

 SmartPoints values per serving 9
SmartPoints values per recipe 9

Takes 15 minutes
Serves 1

130 g skinless chicken breast (see
    Cook's tip)
calorie controlled cooking spray
60 g crusty roll, halved
1 large tomato, sliced thinly
a small handful of wild rocket
salt and freshly ground black pepper

For the herby lemon mayo
2 tablespoons reduced fat mayonnaise
1 tablespoon lemon juice
½ teaspoon Dijon mustard
1 tablespoon chopped mixed fresh
    herbs (e.g. parsley, tarragon and
    chives)

A mighty sandwich that knocks spots off any ready-made shop-bought version.

1. To make the mayonnaise, combine all the ingredients in a bowl, check the seasoning and set aside. Mist the chicken with the cooking spray and season.

2. Preheat a griddle pan until hot. Add the chicken and cook for 8 minutes, turning occasionally, until cooked through. Allow to rest for 2–3 minutes.

3. While the chicken is resting, toast the cut sides of the roll on the griddle pan. Spread the bottom half with the mayonnaise, then top with the chicken and tomato. Scatter with rocket and top with the other half of the roll. Serve immediately.

GF For a gluten free version, simply swap the crusty roll for a gluten free crusty roll, for a total of 9 **SmartPoints** values.

🍴 COOK'S TIP While it is important to cook chicken thoroughly (make sure there is no pink meat and that the juices run clear), try not to overcook it as the result will be tough and dry. Instead, fry until just cooked through then allow to rest for a couple of minutes before serving – it really does make a difference. To prepare the chicken breast for this recipe, simply place between two sheets of cling film and flatten to about 0.5 cm thick using a rolling pin.

BALSAMIC LEEK AND
goat's cheese TARTS

 4 SmartPoints values per serving 4
SmartPoints values per recipe 21

 Takes 45 minutes
Serves 6

350 g baby leeks, trimmed and sliced
2 teaspoons fresh thyme leaves, plus
    a few sprigs to garnish
2 teaspoons lemon juice
1 tablespoon balsamic vinegar
3 sheets filo pastry
20 g low fat spread, melted
70 g goat's cheese with rind, sliced into
    6 discs
salt and freshly ground black pepper

Serve these with a nice salad for a great sit-down lunch.

1. Preheat the oven to Gas Mark 6/200°C/fan oven 180°C. Put the leeks, thyme leaves and lemon juice in a large, heavy based pan with 3 tablespoons cold water. Season and cook gently, uncovered, for 15 minutes, stirring occasionally, until the leeks have softened – add a splash more water if they start to stick. Stir in the balsamic vinegar, then cook, half-covered, for 15–20 minutes, stirring occasionally, until the leeks are completely soft and starting to break up.

2. Meanwhile, cut each filo sheet in half to make a total of 6 squares. Use half of the low fat spread to lightly grease the inside of 6 small loose-bottomed tart tins. Brush a piece of filo with a little of the remaining melted spread, then press into one of the tins, brushed side up, scrunching the edges of the filo to fit inside the tin. Repeat with the remaining filo and tins until the pastry and spread is all used up. Put the tins on to a baking sheet and bake for 3–4 minutes until pale golden.

3. Divide the leek mixture between the tarts and top each with a goat's cheese disc. Turn the oven down to Gas Mark 5/190°C/fan oven 170°C. Return the tarts to the oven for 10 minutes until the pastry is golden and the cheese has started to melt. Carefully remove the tarts from the tins, then serve each topped with a small thyme sprig.

CHECK OUT WHEN LEEKS ARE IN
SEASON ON PAGES 10–11.

SPICY *barbecued* FISH WRAPS

 SmartPoints values per recipe 5
SmartPoints values per recipe 25

Takes 30 minutes
Serves 6

3 x 100 g coley fillets, defrosted
   if frozen
1 tablespoon runny honey
1 teaspoon Cajun spice mix
3 teaspoons lime juice
3 tablespoons reduced fat mayonnaise
2 heaped tablespoons chopped
   fresh coriander
3 x 40 g wholemeal tortilla wraps
a large handful of watercress or rocket
salt and freshly ground black pepper
lime wedges, to serve

What could be simpler than throwing your fish fillet on the barbie and then rolling it in a wrap to eat straight away?

1. If the fish has been frozen, pat it dry with kitchen paper. Mix the honey, spice and 1 teaspoon of the lime juice into a paste, then smear all over the fish. Place the fish in a plastic sandwich or freezer bag and keep chilled until ready to cook.

2. Combine the mayonnaise, coriander and remaining lime juice, season and store in a small pot or jam jar. Keep the mayo mixture chilled until ready to serve.

3. Cook the fish over medium coals or place under a hot grill for 10–12 minutes until nicely charred, with the flesh just starting to flake.

4. Warm the wraps on the barbecue or in the oven and spread each with 1 tablespoon of the lime mayonnaise. Add some watercress or rocket and the fish and wrap tightly. Cut each wrap in half and pop a lime wedge on top to serve.

HERBS AND SPICES ARE A GREAT KITCHEN STAPLE – CHECK OUT SOME OTHER HANDY KITCHEN ESSENTIALS ON PAGES 12–13.

MUST-TRY BROAD BEAN
bruschetta

 **SmartPoints** values per serving 6
SmartPoints values per recipe 6

V

Takes 30 minutes
Serves 1

1 Weight Watchers petit pain (or similar)
100 g broad beans, podded
1 tablespoon fresh mint leaves, torn
zest and juice of ½ small lemon
1 small garlic clove
20 g medium fat soft goat's cheese,
    chopped
salt and freshly ground black pepper

**Bruschetta is Italian 'toast' and makes an ideal light lunch –
this version is topped with minty crushed broad beans.**

1. Preheat the oven to Gas Mark 6/200°C/fan oven 180°C. Bake the
petit pain for 8 minutes, then split it open and bake for 5 minutes, or
until golden. Meanwhile, boil the beans for 5 minutes, or until tender.

2. Drain the beans, refresh under cold water and pop them from their
grey skins. Place them in a bowl with the mint and lemon juice and
roughly crush with a fork. Season.

3. Rub the petit pain with the garlic clove and top with the bean
mixture. Scatter over the goat's cheese and lemon zest, and serve.

QUICK kitchen workout

Pasta on to boil? Ragù simmering away in the pan? Then why not have a go at these quick kitchen exercises while you're waiting? Complete each exercise for 30 seconds, one after the other, for 1 circuit. Remember to rest for 30 seconds between each exercise!

WHAT YOU'LL NEED • A KITCHEN OR DINING CHAIR • 2 CANS OF TOMATOES (OR SIMILAR) OR 2 DUMBBELLS

TRICEPS DIPS ON CHAIR
TARGET AREA: **ARMS**

Grab a kitchen chair, about the height of the one in the picture, and with your feet hip-width apart and your knees bent, support your body weight with both hands behind you. Bend at the elbows as you lower your bottom to just above the floor. Keep your back straight and close to your hands at all times. Straighten your elbows in between each dip to return to the starting position.
Tip: to step it up, extend your legs straight out in front of you.

WALKING LUNGES
TARGET AREA: **LEGS**

Stand with your back straight, legs shoulder-width apart and hands on hips. If using dumbbells or cans, hold them by your sides. Leading with your right heel, take a big step forward and lunge down, bending both legs. Make sure your front knee is above your ankle so your leg is at 90 degrees, and your back knee hovers just above the floor. Push up through your right heel and come back up to standing. Take a big step forward, leading with your left heel, and lunge. Keep lunging forward in an exaggerated walk, or lunge on the spot. Keep your hips facing forwards.

SQUATS

TARGET AREA: LEGS AND GLUTES

Stand with your feet parallel and directly underneath your shoulders. Hold your arms out in front of you. Bend your knees towards a 90-degree angle and lower your bottom as if you were about to sit back into a chair. Keep your weight evenly distributed through your heels and keep your knees above your feet. Squeeze your bottom on the way back up and push through your heels as you straighten your legs in between each squat.

PEC DECK

TARGET AREA: ARMS AND CHEST

Grab your dumbbells or cans of tomatoes. Holding a can or weight in each hand in front of you, begin with your elbows at shoulder height and bent at a 90-degree angle. Squeeze your chest muscles as you slowly bring your elbows in towards each other, making sure they remain at shoulder height. Slowly return the elbows back out to the starting position, keeping your chin tucked in throughout the exercise.

OUTWARD ROTATIONS

TARGET AREA: ARMS AND BACK

Keeping hold of your cans or dumbbells, stand with your feet hip-distance apart and knees slightly bent. Bring your hands together in front of you. Bend the elbows at 90 degrees with your palms facing up. Keep your shoulders back and down as you take the hands apart and out to the side, squeezing the shoulderblades together. Tip: keep your elbows tucked in by your sides at all times and keep the movement slow and controlled.

5 TRIED AND TESTED WAYS TO exercise in disguise

Mastered the quick kitchen workout? Here are some other ways to move more without even thinking about it.

1 CLEAN UP!
Wash windows, mop floors and scrub the tub – make housework less of a chore and think of the benefits. And if the weather is nice get out and channel your inner Titchmarsh; make your garden beautiful while getting fit.

2 WALK LIKE YOU'RE LATE.
Swing your arms, pull your tummy in and squeeze your bum cheeks for maximum effect. It'll soon become second nature and you'll be doing it without even thinking about it.

3 TAKE THE STAIRS.
Use the stairs instead of lifts or escalators whenever possible. But take the steps one at a time, not two. Researchers have found more calories are burned this way.

4 IT'S AN OLDIE BUT GOODIE.
Get off the bus one stop early. If you commute to work, this is perfect. Don't spend the entire journey sitting on a bus stuck in a traffic jam – work your legs, walk the rest of the way and breathe in the fresh air.

5 WEAR AN ACTIVITY DEVICE.
These brilliant gadgets count your daily steps and can be cheap and easy to use. Keep track of how active you are and gradually build up your steps each day. Some devices are app based and will even let you hold challenges with other users; friendly ones, of course – no running around the living room at one minute to midnight in a desperate attempt to win the challenge!

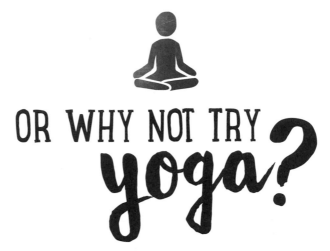

OR WHY NOT TRY yoga?

If you think it's not for you then think again. You don't have to be a contortionist to enjoy the benefits it offers and you certainly don't have to have trained with a swami in the highest peaks of the Himalayas. All you need is 20 minutes of your day, some floor space and a 'can do' attitude, and you're good to go.

SOME HELPFUL TIPS:

YOU DON'T HAVE TO HAVE ALL THE KIT TO ENJOY YOGA.
It does help to wear loose-fitting clothing as this means you can move more easily. And don't spend a fortune on a yoga mat; if you don't have one, a towel will do. Follow a DVD or find an online class if you want to try yoga at home. If you're hoping to get out and meet people and would prefer a group class then find one local to home or your workplace.

MAKE TIME FOR YOURSELF.
If you're practising yoga at home then make your session a regular thing and if you join a class then make sure you can get there in time and don't have to rush out the door halfway through.

GO AT YOUR OWN PACE.
Don't go into it thinking you need to master all of the postures in your first session (you'll end up a bit like Bambi taking his first steps!). It will take time.

STOP THINKING!
It's hard when you're constantly wondering what to cook the kids for dinner or what tomorrow might bring, but yoga is about the present and when you calm your mind (this will also take time to learn), you'll experience the benefits of focusing on the 'now'.

let's start
a salad
revolution

spiced duck
AND GRAPEFRUIT SALAD

 SmartPoints values per serving 6
SmartPoints values per recipe 12

 Takes 20 minutes
Serves 2

2 x 150 g skinless duck breasts, at
    room temperature
1 teaspoon Chinese five spice
2 teaspoons extra virgin olive oil
½ teaspoon runny honey
¼ teaspoon English mustard powder
½ teaspoon wholegrain mustard
1 large pink grapefruit, segmented,
    juice reserved
100 g mixed salad leaves
1 small red onion, sliced thinly
4 tablespoons pomegranate seeds

**A great citrusy lunch dish – or divide it into four portions for a
dinner party starter.**

1. Preheat the oven to Gas Mark 6/200°C/fan oven 180°C. Dust the
duck with the Chinese five spice. Heat 1 teaspoon of the olive oil in a
frying pan and cook the duck for 5 minutes until brown all over.

2. Place the duck breasts on a baking tray and cook in the oven for
10 minutes. Remove from the oven, cover and leave to rest for
5 minutes before slicing.

3. Combine the remaining olive oil, honey, mustards and juice from
the grapefruit to make the dressing. Divide the salad leaves between
2 plates and top with the duck slices and grapefruit segments.
Scatter over the onion and pomegranate seeds and serve drizzled
with the dressing.

THAI CHICKEN *salad*

SmartPoints values per serving 5
SmartPoints values per recipe 10

Takes 20 minutes
Serves 2

65 g fine rice noodles
250 g skinless chicken breast, cut
    into strips
calorie controlled cooking spray
75 g baby corn, halved
60 g mangetout or sugar snap peas
50 g carrots, cut into ribbons
2 heaped tablespoons chopped
    fresh coriander
1 heaped tablespoon each chopped
    fresh mint and basil

For the dressing
2 tablespoons soy sauce
1 teaspoon Thai fish sauce
juice of 1 lime
2 crushed garlic cloves
1 large mild red chilli, diced (or sliced
    bird's-eye chillies for authentic heat)
1 teaspoon finely grated fresh
    root ginger
½ teaspoon honey

Colourful and aromatic, this quick salad is one you're sure to want to make time and time again.

1. Place the noodles in a heatproof bowl and cover with boiling water. Let them stand for 5 minutes, or until just soft, then drain.

2. Mix together all the ingredients for the dressing. Stir half of the dressing through the noodles and pour the remainder over the chicken strips in a shallow bowl.

3. Heat a wok over a high heat and spray with the cooking spray. Add the corn and stir-fry for 2 minutes, then add the mangetout or sugar snap peas. Stir-fry for a further 2 minutes, adding the carrots for the last 30 seconds. Add the vegetables to the noodles.

4. Heat the wok again then add the chicken strips and their marinade. Cook, stirring occasionally, for 3–4 minutes until cooked through. Add most of the herbs to the noodles and toss everything together, mixing well, then divide between 2 plates or bowls. Top with the chicken and remaining herbs and serve.

COOK'S TIP This salad is good cold, too. Rinse the noodles in cold water and let the vegetables and chicken cool before mixing everything together in a bowl then cover and chill. Make sure to eat it within 24 hours.

chicken Caesar
WITH PEAR AND WALNUTS

 SmartPoints values per serving 6
SmartPoints values per recipe 6

Takes 10 minutes
Serves 1

40 g wholemeal bread cubes
30 g 0% fat natural yogurt
1 teaspoon wholegrain or Dijon mustard
1 small pear or apple, chopped
lemon juice
50 g Cos lettuce, shredded
a handful of watercress
60 g cooked skinless chicken breast, shredded
10 g Parmesan cheese, grated
5 g walnuts
freshly ground black pepper

An iconic main-meal salad you can whip up in minutes.

1. Dry-fry the wholemeal bread cubes for 3–5 minutes, turning regularly until toasted, then set aside. Combine the yogurt and wholegrain or Dijon mustard with some black pepper.

2. Toss the chopped pear or apple in a little lemon juice. Arrange the Cos lettuce and watercress in a serving bowl and scatter over the chopped apple or pear. Top with the shredded chicken breast, the wholemeal croûtons and the grated Parmesan. Sprinkle the walnuts on top and drizzle the yogurt dressing over.

GF Replace the wholemeal bread cubes with gluten free wholemeal bread for a total of 7 **SmartPoints** values.

GRIDDLED CHICKEN SALAD WITH
asparagus AND PARMESAN

 SmartPoints values per serving 8
SmartPoints values per recipe 16

Takes 20 minutes
Serves 2

calorie controlled cooking spray
2 x 150 g skinless chicken breasts,
    each sliced into 5 diagonally
2 x 40 g slices ciabatta (baked if
    part-baked)
1 garlic clove, halved (optional)
250 g asparagus, trimmed
2 bunches of cherry tomatoes on
    the vine
1 Little Gem lettuce, leaves separated
25 g wild rocket
2 teaspoons extra virgin olive oil
½ tablespoon balsamic vinegar
30 g Parmesan cheese shavings
salt and freshly ground black pepper

So quick and easy – charred asparagus and griddled chicken make a heavenly match in this sensational supper salad.

1. Preheat the grill and line the grill pan with foil. Heat a griddle pan and mist with the cooking spray. Griddle the chicken strips for 5–6 minutes until just cooked through, then season and leave to rest for a few minutes on a plate. Meanwhile, mist the pan again and griddle the ciabatta slices to toast them (do this in the toaster if you prefer). Rub with the cut garlic clove, if using.

2. Lay the asparagus and tomatoes on the grill pan, season and mist with cooking spray. Grill for 5–6 minutes, turning the asparagus once, until tender and charred.

3. Toss the Little Gem and rocket with the olive oil and balsamic vinegar, then divide between 2 shallow serving bowls. Scatter with the asparagus, tomatoes, chicken strips and Parmesan shavings and serve with the garlic toast.

 Swap the ciabatta for a gluten free version for 8 **SmartPoints** values.

SIMPLE STEAK AND
roast butternut
SALAD

 5 SmartPoints values per serving 5
SmartPoints values per recipe 10

 Takes 30 minutes
Serves 2

 GF

300–350 g butternut squash, cut into
    bite-size pieces
5 small shallots, peeled and halved
a pinch of dried red chilli flakes
2 x 100 g lean sirloin steaks
2 teaspoons olive oil
100 g mixed leaves, e.g. pea shoots
    and rocket
1 teaspoon extra virgin olive oil
juice of ½ lemon
salt and freshly ground black pepper

A seriously good steak salad. The pea shoots are tasty and so pretty!

1. Preheat the oven to Gas Mark 6/200°C/fan oven 180°C. Place the squash and shallots in a roasting tray, season and sprinkle with the chilli flakes. Rub the steaks with a little of the olive oil and set aside. Drizzle the rest over the vegetables. Roast for 25 minutes, or until soft and starting to char.

2. When the vegetables are nearly ready, heat a small non-stick frying pan and add the steaks. Sear for 2–3 minutes on each side, or until done to your liking. Place on a plate, season and leave to rest for a few minutes.

3. Place the salad leaves in a serving bowl, season and toss with the extra virgin olive oil and lemon juice. Slice the steak into strips, then add to the salad, along with the roasted squash and shallots, and serve.

THAI BEEF
lettuce cups

SmartPoints values per serving 3
SmartPoints values per recipe 10

 Takes 15 minutes
Makes 8 (2 cups each)

½ firm (under-ripe) mango
75 g cucumber
a handful of fresh coriander leaves
a small handful of fresh mint leaves,
    chopped roughly, or smaller leaves
    left whole
2 Little Gem lettuces
160 g beef fillet
¼ teaspoon olive oil
salt and freshly ground black pepper
15 g chopped roasted peanuts,
    to garnish

For the dressing
1 teaspoon palm sugar (or soft brown
    sugar)
1 teaspoon lime juice
1 small garlic clove, crushed
1 teaspoon finely grated fresh
    root ginger
1 teaspoon Thai fish sauce
½ long thin red chilli, sliced finely
    (remove the seeds if you prefer)

**A really easy sharing starter you can serve in minutes.
The combination of spicy meat and cool, crisp veg is
typically Thai.**

1. Remove the skin from the mango and cut the flesh into matchsticks.
Cut the cucumber into matchsticks as well, then toss together in a bowl
with the coriander and mint. (Make sure all the ingredients are nice
and dry – if necessary, pat with a paper towel before combining.)

2. Whisk all the dressing ingredients together, reserving a little of the
chilli to garnish. Set aside.

3. Pick 8 nicely curved, medium-sized leaves from the lettuces. Wash
and pat them dry, then arrange on a serving platter.

4. Heat a small griddle or frying pan. Rub the beef with the olive oil.
When the pan is really hot, sear the beef for 2 minutes on each side.
Season and set aside to rest.

5. Drizzle the dressing over the salad and toss lightly, then divide
between the lettuce cups. Slice the beef thinly and arrange on top of
the salad, then scatter with the chopped peanuts and reserved chilli.
Serve immediately.

SWEET POTATO, BULGUR WHEAT AND *prosciutto* SALAD

 SmartPoints values per serving 8
SmartPoints values per recipe 32

Takes 30 minutes
Serves 4

150 g bulgur wheat
400 g sweet potatoes, peeled and cut
    into 1 cm cubes
2 teaspoons olive oil
4 tablespoons torn fresh basil
2 tablespoons chopped fresh parsley
½ lemon
50 g wild rocket
70 g prosciutto slices, torn
25 g pecorino cheese, shaved
salt and freshly ground black pepper

The mix of textures and sweet-salty flavours makes this a dish to satisfy the senses.

1. Preheat the oven to Gas Mark 7/220ºC/fan oven 200ºC. Place the bulgur wheat in a large bowl, cover it with boiling water and leave it to absorb the water for 20 minutes.

2. Meanwhile, place the sweet potatoes in a roasting tin, drizzle with 1 teaspoon of the olive oil and season well. Roast for 20 minutes, or until lightly charred, turning occasionally. Drain the bulgur wheat well, pressing out any excess moisture, and combine it with the sweet potatoes. Add the basil, parsley and a squeeze of lemon juice and season well.

3. Put the remaining olive oil in a mixing bowl with another squeeze of lemon juice and season. Add the rocket, prosciutto and pecorino to the bowl and combine well, using your hands. Arrange the bulgur wheat and sweet potatoes on a serving dish and top with the prosciutto, pecorino and rocket. Serve.

¶ COOK'S TIP Prosciutto is an Italian ham that has been seasoned, cured and air-dried. You can eat it straight from the packet or pan-fry it to give a dry, crispy texture.

farfalle WITH PRAWNS, WATERCRESS AND CAPERS

 SmartPoints values per serving 7
SmartPoints values per recipe 14

Takes 15 minutes
Serves 2

100 g farfalle pasta
4 spring onions, sliced finely
25 g watercress
200 g small vine tomatoes, halved
    or quartered
150 g cooked peeled prawns
lemon wedges, to serve (optional)

For the dressing

1 tablespoon capers, rinsed, plus 1
    teaspoon extra to garnish (optional)
2 tablespoons chopped fresh dill
1 tablespoon lemon juice
2 tablespoons reduced fat mayonnaise
freshly ground black pepper

A delicious summery pasta salad, ideal for al fresco eating.

1. Cook the pasta according to the packet instructions, then drain and refresh under cold running water. Drain very well and tip into a mixing bowl. Add the spring onions, watercress, tomatoes and prawns.

2. To make the dressing, blot the capers with kitchen paper, then chop them roughly. Combine with the remaining ingredients and season well with black pepper. Add a splash of water if the mixture looks too thick.

3. Divide the pasta between 2 bowls and drizzle with the dressing, then sprinkle with extra capers if you like. Serve with the lemon wedges, if using.

> **COOK'S TIP** If you make this the night before, you can take a portion to work. Mix the dressing into the salad, and just pop a lemon wedge in your lunch box to squeeze over when ready to eat.

SIMPLY LOVELY *rice paper* PRAWN ROLLS

 SmartPoints values per serving 7
SmartPoints values per recipe 26

 Takes 30 minutes
Serves 4

50 g Thai rice noodles
50 g beansprouts
1 carrot, halved and cut into very
    fine matchsticks
4 spring onions, halved and sliced
200 g peeled and cooked prawns,
    defrosted if frozen
3 tablespoons chopped fresh basil
1 teaspoon Thai fish sauce
zest of 1 lime
8 x 22 cm rice papers

For the dipping sauce
Juice of 2 limes
2 tablespoons Thai fish sauce
½ red chilli, de-seeded and chopped
    very finely
1 tablespoon brown sugar
2 tablespoons torn fresh coriander
1 tablespoon mirin or medium sherry
1 garlic clove, crushed

Delicate rice paper parcels encase Thai-style veg and succulent prawns.

1. Combine the ingredients for the dipping sauce with 2 tablespoons water and set to one side. Place the rice noodles in a bowl and cover with boiling water. Stir and soak for about 5 minutes, or until tender. Refresh under cold water and drain well before placing in a bowl.

2. Add the beansprouts, carrot, spring onions, prawns, basil, fish sauce and lime zest. Combine well and set aside.

3. Fill a bowl wide enough to fit a whole rice paper with cold water and add one of the rice papers. Carefully dunk under the water for a couple of minutes until completely softened. Shake dry, then place on a clean tea towel on the work surface.

4. Spoon an eighth of the filling in a mound along the centre of the rice paper circle, leaving a 4 cm gap at each end. Fold the sides over the filling and then roll up into a tube shape similar to a spring roll. Set to one side and repeat with the remaining rice papers. Serve with the dipping sauce.

COOK'S TIP You can buy rice paper pancakes in Asian supermarkets. If you haven't got one near you, look online.

SESAME AND LIME
tuna salad

7 SmartPoints values per serving 7
SmartPoints values per recipe 7

GF **Takes 25 minutes**
Serves 1

zest and juice of ½ lime
½ teaspoon brown sugar
30 g brown rice, cooked and cooled
    under running water
2 teaspoons soy sauce
1 teaspoon toasted sesame oil
½ small red pepper, chopped
80 g can tuna in brine, drained
a handful of chopped fresh coriander
lime wedge, to serve

Perfect for picnics, too, or for taking to work in a lunchbox.

1. Combine the juice and sugar and stir into the rice with the soy sauce, lime zest, oil and pepper. Cool thoroughly, then cover and store in the fridge until ready to serve.

2. Stir in the tuna and coriander, serve with a lime wedge and enjoy.

> **COOK'S TIP** The rice can be prepared the day ahead and kept in the fridge overnight. Just add the tuna and coriander when you are ready to eat or before you head off to work.

GOAT'S CHEESE, PARMA HAM AND *strawberry* SALAD

 10 SmartPoints value

SmartPoints values per serving 10
SmartPoints values per recipe 10

Takes 5 minutes
Serves 1

2 x 17 g slices Parma ham
2 handfuls of peppery salad leaves
40 g goat's cheese, sliced
40 g ripe strawberries, sliced
1 tablespoon balsamic vinegar
35 g slice granary bread

A mixture of textures and flavours that works surprisingly well. Go on – give it a try!

1. Arrange the slices of Parma ham on a plate with the peppery salad leaves, goat's cheese and strawberries. Dress with the balsamic vinegar and serve with the granary bread.

GF For a gluten free version, swap the granary bread for a 35 g slice of gluten free brown bread for a total of 10 **SmartPoints** values.

SUPER-EASY *panzanella*

 SmartPoints values per serving 6
SmartPoints values per recipe 6

V **Takes 10 minutes + standing**
Serves 1

40 g slice wholemeal bread
1 garlic clove, halved
5 g pine nuts
75 g vine tomatoes, chopped
½ red pepper, chopped
½ red onion, sliced
40 g cucumber, diced
1 tablespoon capers
a small handful of fresh basil leaves,
    plus extra to garnish (optional)
a handful of rocket, to serve

For the dressing
1 teaspoon olive oil
a squeeze of lemon juice
2 teaspoons balsamic vinegar
salt and freshly ground black pepper

What better way to enjoy the fresh taste of an Italian summer? Panzanella is a traditional Tuscan salad of bread and sun-ripened tomatoes, which is ideal for a packed lunch.

1. Toast the wholemeal bread, rub with the cut side of the garlic clove, then tear into pieces.

2. Dry-fry the pine nuts in a small non-stick pan for 1–2 minutes until golden all over, then set aside.

3. Combine the bread and the tomatoes in a bowl, gently squashing the tomatoes so that the juices are released. Stir in the pepper, onion, cucumber, capers and basil.

4. Whisk together the olive oil, lemon juice and balsamic vinegar and season. Pour over the salad. Stir well and set aside for 20 minutes to allow the bread to soak up the dressing.

5. Scatter over the pine nuts, and serve with rocket and some extra basil leaves, if using.

a really pretty
COURGETTE AND MINT SALAD

3 SmartPoints values per serving 3
SmartPoints values per recipe 12

Takes 30 minutes
Serves 4

V

2 courgettes, cut in ribbons
calorie controlled cooking spray
75 g wholewheat couscous, soaked
    in boiling water according to the
    packet instructions
a small bunch of fresh mint, chopped
    roughly
a small bunch of fresh parsley, chopped
    roughly
3 spring onions, sliced finely
2 green peppers, de-seeded and diced
200 g cherry tomatoes, quartered
juice of 1 lemon
1 tablespoon olive oil
2 tablespoons pomegranate seeds
salt and freshly ground black pepper

This vibrant salad is great on its own or eaten alongside grilled or barbecued meat or fish.

1. Mist the courgette slices with the cooking spray and heat a griddle pan to hot. Griddle until lightly charred, then set aside to cool.

2. Fork the soaked couscous to fluff it up, then add the herbs, spring onions, peppers and tomatoes and toss well.

3. Mix the lemon juice with the olive oil and some seasoning. Pour over the couscous and mix through. Add the griddled courgettes and serve with the pomegranate seeds on top.

QUICK *feta* AND *watermelon* SALAD

SmartPoints values per serving 9
SmartPoints values per recipe 9

GF

Takes 10 minutes
Serves 1

V

40 g feta cheese, cubed
100 g cooked brown rice
50 g cucumber, diced
50 g watermelon, cut into chunks

For the dressing
50 g low fat natural yogurt
1 tablespoon chopped fresh mint

Although it sounds like an unusual combination this salad tastes delicious – the tangy feta and the sweet watermelon work really well together. A great take-to-work option.

1. Mix together the feta cheese, brown rice, cucumber and chunks of watermelon.

2. Combine the natural yogurt with the chopped mint and serve it with the salad.

REALLY EASY ASPARAGUS WITH *griddled* HALLOUMI

9 SmartPoints values per serving 9
SmartPoints values per recipe 18

Takes 10 minutes
Serves 2

1 bunch of asparagus (approx 350 g),
   woody ends snapped off
juice of ½ lemon
150 g light halloumi cheese, cut into
   4 thick slices
3 teaspoons extra virgin olive oil
1 tablespoon capers, drained and
   chopped
1 tablespoon chopped fresh
   parsley
freshly ground black pepper

A quick and impressive light lunch, perfect for al fresco dining – especially when asparagus is in season (see the guide on pages 10–11).

1. Steam the asparagus spears for 3–4 minutes until tender. Divide between 2 warmed plates and season with a little of the lemon juice and some cracked black pepper.

2. Meanwhile, heat a griddle pan. Brush the halloumi slices with 1 teaspoon of the olive oil. Griddle for a minute or two on each side, or until softened with nice griddle lines. Place 2 slices on top of each plate of asparagus.

3. Mix the chopped capers and parsley together and sprinkle over the asparagus and halloumi. Squeeze over a little more lemon and add some more black pepper, then drizzle each plate with 1 teaspoon olive oil. Serve immediately.

gorgeous LENTIL SALAD WITH GOAT'S CHEESE AND ROASTED PEPPERS

SmartPoints values per serving 6
SmartPoints values per recipe 35

**Preparation time 20 minutes
+ soaking
Cooking time 40 minutes
Serves 6**

200 g dried green lentils, soaked for
    30 minutes
1 red onion, sliced thinly
1 tablespoon red wine vinegar
4 teaspoons extra virgin olive oil
1 garlic clove, sliced finely
a small bunch of fresh parsley, chopped
2 tablespoons chopped fresh chives
½ small bunch of fresh mint, chopped
120 g goat's cheese, chopped
salt and freshly ground black pepper

For the roasted peppers and tomatoes
300 g baby plum tomatoes, halved
3 red peppers, de-seeded and
    quartered
4 sprigs of fresh thyme
calorie controlled cooking spray
2 tablespoons balsamic vinegar
sea salt

Green lentils hold their shape when cooked, making them ideal for a range of dishes including this mouthwatering salad.

1. Preheat the oven to Gas Mark 4/180°C/fan oven 160°C. Place the tomatoes and peppers skin side down on a large baking sheet and top with the thyme sprigs. Mist with the cooking spray, drizzle with the balsamic vinegar and add a good sprinkling of sea salt. Put in the oven to roast for 40 minutes, then set aside to cool.

2. Meanwhile, cook the lentils according to the packet instructions, then drain and leave to cool slightly.

3. In a small bowl, mix the red onion with the red wine vinegar, olive oil and garlic and then pour over the lentils and mix well. Next, add the chopped herbs and season.

4. Serve the lentils with the tomatoes and peppers mixed in and the goat's cheese scattered on top.

VARIATION Don't like goat's cheese? Substitute the same amount of light feta cheese for a **SmartPoints** value of 5 per serving.

¶¶ COOK'S TIP Store the cooked lentils in an airtight container in the fridge and add the peppers and tomatoes when ready to serve with the goat's cheese.

GOT SOME TIME WAITING FOR THE LENTILS TO COOK? CHECK OUT OUR QUICK KITCHEN WORKOUT ON PAGES 48-9 TO GET MOVING WHILE YOU'RE COOKING.

all of your
favourites

LAMB *meatballs* AND AUBERGINE IN TOMATO SAUCE

 **SmartPoints** values per serving 7
SmartPoints values per recipe 26

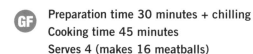 Preparation time 30 minutes + chilling
Cooking time 45 minutes
Serves 4 (makes 16 meatballs)

1 aubergine, cut into large chunks
calorie controlled cooking spray
salt and freshly ground black pepper
a small bunch of chopped fresh parsley,
    to serve

For the meatballs
40 g bulgur wheat
350 g lean (less than 16% fat) lamb
    mince
½ onion, grated finely
2 garlic cloves, crushed
2 teaspoons ground cumin
½ teaspoon ground cinnamon
a handful of chopped fresh parsley

For the sauce
1 onion, chopped
1 teaspoon olive oil
2 garlic cloves, crushed
3 sprigs of fresh thyme
1 bay leaf
400 g can chopped tomatoes
2 tablespoons tomato purée
250 ml vegetable stock (see page 220)

Minced lamb and aubergine are typical ingredients in Greek cuisine and these tasty meatballs have a distinct flavour of the Mediterranean.

1. Preheat the oven to Gas Mark 6/200°C/fan oven 180°C. Put the aubergine on a baking tray and mist with the cooking spray. Roast for 20 minutes, or until soft.

2. Meanwhile, cover the bulgur wheat with boiling water and leave to absorb for 5 minutes. Put all the remaining meatball ingredients into a bowl, season and knead together. Drain the bulgur wheat, add to the bowl and mix well. Next, take golf ball-sized portions of the mixture and roll into 16 meatballs. Chill on a plate for 30 minutes.

3. To make the sauce, fry the onion in the oil until lightly coloured. Add the garlic and continue to fry. Next, add the herbs and tomatoes, followed by the tomato purée and vegetable stock. Bring the sauce to the boil and season.

4. Brown the meatballs in a frying pan misted with cooking spray before adding them to the sauce and simmering for 30 minutes. Stir in the aubergine 15 minutes before the end of the cooking time. Just before serving, add the chopped parsley.

CHECK OUT OUR SEASONAL FOODS GUIDE ON PAGES 10–11 TO SEE WHEN AUBERGINES ARE IN SEASON.

BEEF RAGÙ WITH
tagliatelle

SmartPoints values per serving 10
SmartPoints values per recipe 38

Preparation time 20 minutes
Cooking time 45 minutes
Serves 4

For the ragù
400 g extra lean (5% fat) beef mince
1 teaspoon olive oil
1 onion, chopped finely
2 carrots, diced finely
2 celery sticks, chopped finely
4 garlic cloves, chopped
½ teaspoon dried oregano
1 bay leaf
400 g can chopped tomatoes
2 tablespoons tomato purée
½ teaspoon sugar
salt and freshly ground black pepper

250 g tagliatelle

This rich-tasting ragù is a slow-cooked sensation. Serve with 15 g grated Parmesan cheese for an extra 2 SmartPoints values per serving.

1. To make the ragù, heat a large non-stick frying pan until hot. Add the mince and cook over a high heat for 5 minutes, stirring and breaking up the meat as it cooks. Tip into a large saucepan. Heat the oil in the same frying pan, add the onion, carrots and celery and cook over a low heat for 10 minutes, or until perfectly softened. Add a splash of water if needed.

2. Stir in the garlic and oregano and cook for 2 minutes. Transfer the mixture to the saucepan, add the remaining ingredients and stir in 500 ml water. Season well, bring to the boil and then simmer for 45 minutes, stirring occasionally, until very rich and thickened.

3. When the ragù is ready, cook the pasta according to the packet instructions and drain. Divide among 4 warmed, shallow bowls and top with the sauce.

🍴 COOK'S TIP This sauce is perfect for freezing. Simply cool quickly, spoon into freezer bags and seal before freezing for up to 3 months. Allow the sauce to defrost thoroughly before simmering until piping hot.

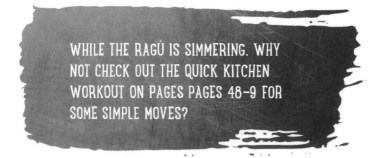

WHILE THE RAGÙ IS SIMMERING. WHY NOT CHECK OUT THE QUICK KITCHEN WORKOUT ON PAGES PAGES 48–9 FOR SOME SIMPLE MOVES?

COCONUT AND GINGER
beef curry

SmartPoints values per serving 11
SmartPoints values per recipe 43

Preparation time 20 minutes
Cooking time 1 hour 20 minutes
Serves 4

calorie controlled cooking spray
600 g lean braising steak, cut into
   large chunks
300 g shallots, chopped finely
4 garlic cloves, chopped
1 tablespoon chopped fresh root ginger
2 teaspoons cumin seeds, crushed
   lightly
10 curry leaves
½ cinnamon stick
6 cardamom pods
4 whole cloves
1 tablespoon medium curry paste
200 ml light coconut milk
150 g trimmed fine green beans
100 g dried basmati rice
100 g peas
150 g cherry tomatoes, halved
1–2 tablespoons light soy sauce
6 tablespoons chopped fresh coriander

A fragrant curry dish that's full of spice but not too hot!

1. Mist a large non-stick frying pan with the cooking spray. Add the beef and fry in batches until well browned. Set to one side. Add the shallots and cook for 10 minutes until softened and coloured. Add the garlic and ginger, all the spices and the curry paste. Cook for 2–3 minutes until fragrant.

2. Return the beef to the pan and stir in the coconut milk along with 250 ml water. Bring almost to the boil, then cover and simmer for 1 hour until the beef is tender. Stir in the beans and cook, uncovered, for 15 minutes until tender.

3. Meanwhile, cook the rice according to the packet instructions. Add the peas and tomatoes to the curry and cook for a further 5 minutes. Season with the soy sauce and half the coriander. Serve spooned over the rice and scattered with the remaining coriander.

COOK'S TIP To freeze the cooked curry, omit the coriander at the end. Allow to cool and cover with a tight-fitting lid before freezing for up to 1 month. To serve, defrost thoroughly and warm through in a pan until piping hot. Scatter with coriander.

THIS RECIPE USES LOTS OF STORECUPBOARD INGREDIENTS - CHECK OUT PAGES 12-13 FOR MORE ESSENTIALS.

seared steak
WITH SALSA VERDE

 SmartPoints values per serving 10
SmartPoints values per recipe 20

 Takes 45 minutes
Serves 2

200 g waxy potatoes, such as Charlotte, sliced
6–8 garlic cloves in their skins (optional)
calorie controlled cooking spray
1 teaspoon English mustard powder
2 x 150 g fillet steaks (about 2.5 cm thick), visible fat removed
250 g spinach
salt and freshly ground black pepper

For the salsa verde
½ garlic clove, crushed
a handful of fresh parsley
a handful of fresh basil
a small handful of fresh mint
1 heaped teaspoon capers, drained and rinsed
1 cornichon
1 anchovy fillet
¼ teaspoon Dijon mustard
½ teaspoon red wine vinegar
1 tablespoon extra virgin olive oil

Salsa verde – or green sauce – is made with fresh herbs and is great served with meat or fish.

1. For the salsa verde, place the crushed garlic in a mixing bowl. Roughly chop all the herbs together using a large knife. Then add the capers, cornichon and anchovy and chop those too, until everything is finely chopped. Add to the mixing bowl. Stir in the Dijon mustard, vinegar and olive oil. Season and set aside.

2. Preheat the oven to Gas Mark 6/200°C/fan oven 180°C. Place the sliced potatoes and garlic cloves, if using, on a baking sheet. Mist well with the cooking spray and cook for 25 minutes, or until the garlic is soft and the potato slices are crisp and golden.

3. Rub the mustard powder into the steaks. Heat a griddle or frying pan, mist with cooking spray and add the steaks. Cook for 2½ minutes on each side for medium rare, or until done to your liking, then season and set aside on a warmed plate to rest.

4. Wilt the spinach in a hot pan, season, then divide between 2 warmed plates. Place a steak on top and pour over some of the juices. Top each steak with a spoonful of the salsa verde, and serve with the potatoes and garlic.

CLASSIC
lasagne

SmartPoints values per serving 11
SmartPoints values per recipe 63

Preparation time 1 hour
Cooking time 45 minutes
Serves 6

150 g lasagne sheets
50 g Parmesan cheese, grated finely
salt and freshly ground black pepper

For the ragù
1 teaspoon olive oil
500 g extra lean steak mince
100 g pancetta, chopped
1 large onion, chopped finely
2 celery sticks, cubed finely
2 carrots, chopped finely
4 garlic cloves, chopped
600 g canned chopped tomatoes
2 tablespoons tomato purée
1 teaspoon sugar
2 tablespoons chopped fresh oregano
500 ml beef stock, made with a cube

For the white sauce
400 ml skimmed milk
cracked peppercorns
a handful of fresh parsley, leaves
    and stalks
1 bay leaf
2 tablespoons cornflour
1 teaspoon Dijon mustard

The ultimate all-in-one dish. Serve with a crisp green salad for no extra SmartPoints.

1. To make the ragù, heat the oil in a large, lidded, non-stick pan and add the beef. Cook over a medium-high heat for 8–10 minutes, breaking up the meat with a wooden spoon as it cooks. Once the mince is nicely browned, remove it using a slotted spoon and set aside.

2. Cook the pancetta in the same pan for around 5 minutes, or until golden. Remove with a slotted spoon and set aside. Add the onion, celery and carrots to the pan. Cover and cook over a low heat for 10 minutes, or until softened. Add the garlic and cook, uncovered, for 2 minutes.

3. Return the beef and pancetta to the pan and add the tomatoes, tomato purée, sugar, oregano and stock. Bring to the boil and simmer for 30 minutes, or until thickened and rich. Season to taste, taking care not to add too much salt.

4. Meanwhile, make the white sauce: put the milk in a small saucepan with the peppercorns, parsley and bay leaf. Slowly bring just to the boil, then remove from the heat and allow to infuse for 10 minutes before passing through a sieve into a jug to remove the herbs. Return the strained milk to the pan.

5. Mix the cornflour with a splash of cold water into a smooth paste. Pour some of the warmed milk over and whisk. Add this mixture to the milk in the pan and whisk again. Slowly bring to the boil, whisking, until the sauce has the consistency of pouring cream. Remove from the heat, mix in the mustard and season to taste.

6. Preheat the oven to Gas Mark 4/180°C/fan oven 160°C. Spoon half the ragù into a 2-litre lasagne dish and top with a layer of lasagne sheets. Spoon around a third of the white sauce over and top with the remaining ragù. Add a final layer of lasagne sheets and the remaining white sauce. Scatter the Parmesan over and bake for 45 minutes, or until golden and bubbling and the pasta is tender.

ultimate GAMMON AND EGG PIE

 SmartPoints values per serving 10
SmartPoints values per recipe 39

Preparation time 30 minutes
Cooking time 30 minutes
Serves 4

600 g floury potatoes, peeled and cut
      into chunks
1 tablespoon low fat spread
1 teaspoon wholegrain mustard
300 g cooked gammon or ham, cut
      into chunks
2 hard-boiled eggs, chopped
30 g reduced fat mature Cheddar
      cheese, grated
salt and freshly ground black pepper

For the sauce
1 tablespoon plain flour
2 teaspoons low fat spread
300 ml skimmed milk
50 g reduced fat mature Cheddar
      cheese, grated
2 teaspoons wholegrain mustard
2 tablespoons chopped fresh
      parsley

**A really satisfying pie that's sure to be a firm family favourite.
Serve with steamed broccoli or greens and carrots.**

1. Cook the potatoes for 10–15 minutes, or until soft, then mash with the low fat spread and mustard. Season to taste.

2. Meanwhile, preheat the oven to Gas Mark 5/190ºC/fan oven 170ºC. Place the gammon in a medium pie dish and top with the eggs.

3. To make the sauce, put the flour, low fat spread and milk in a small saucepan and bring to the boil, whisking constantly. Turn the heat down and cook for another 5 minutes, stirring often, then remove from the heat and stir in the cheese, mustard and parsley. Season to taste then pour over the ham and eggs.

4. Spoon the mash over the top and scatter with the grated cheese. Bake for 30 minutes until golden and bubbling.

> **Cook's tips** You could get your ham from the deli counter, but a cheaper option is to buy a gammon joint and cook it yourself, then use the leftovers for this lovely pie.
>
> For perfect hard-boiled eggs, place room-temperature eggs in a small saucepan, cover with water and bring to a rolling simmer. Turn the heat down and simmer gently for 7 minutes, then drain and run under cold water to cool.

PORK AND ROSEMARY
stuffed peppers

 SmartPoints values per serving 6
SmartPoints values per recipe 24

Preparation time 25 minutes
Cooking time 40 minutes
Serves 4

calorie controlled cooking spray
1 onion, chopped finely
150 g courgette, chopped finely
1 garlic clove, crushed
450 g extra lean (5% fat) pork mince
1 tablespoon finely chopped fresh
    rosemary
50 g fresh wholegrain breadcrumbs
50 g Parmesan cheese, grated finely
4 red peppers, halved and de-seeded
salt and freshly ground black pepper
rocket and watercress salad, to serve

These colourful stuffed peppers make a fabulous light Mediterranean-style supper.

1. Preheat the oven to Gas Mark 6/200°C/fan oven 180°C. Mist a pan with the cooking spray and add the onion and courgette. Fry, stirring, for 10 minutes, or until softened but not coloured.

2. Add the garlic and fry for a further minute, then stir in the pork mince. Fry, stirring frequently, for 10 minutes, or until browned and any liquid has evaporated.

3. Remove from the heat and stir in the rosemary, breadcrumbs and 30 g of the Parmesan. Season. Arrange the peppers in a large ovenproof dish (or 2 small ones) so that they fit snugly and divide the mince mixture between them. Top with the remaining Parmesan and bake for 40 minutes, or until golden. Serve with the rocket and watercress salad.

GF For a gluten free version, swap the wholegrain breadcrumbs for gluten free breadcrumbs for the same **SmartPoints** values.

best ever TOAD IN THE HOLE WITH MUSTARD GRAVY

 SmartPoints values per serving 11
SmartPoints values per recipe 43

Preparation time 10 minutes
Cooking time 30 minutes
Serves 4

8 low fat sausages
2 tablespoons sunflower oil
300 g shallots, halved if large
6 fresh sage leaves

For the batter
125 g plain flour
2 eggs
200 ml skimmed milk

For the gravy
2 teaspoons gravy granules
1 teaspoon wholegrain mustard

Comfort food at its best! Serve with steamed green vegetables of your choice, for a meal that ticks all the boxes.

1. Preheat the oven to Gas Mark 6/200°C/fan oven 180°C. Preheat the grill to medium-high and cook the sausages for 15 minutes, turning occasionally, until cooked through. Whisk together the batter ingredients and set aside in the fridge until needed.

2. Heat a large non-stick frying pan with ½ tablespoon of the oil, then add the shallots. Cook over a medium heat for 10 minutes until softened and golden. Pour the remaining oil into a 23 cm square roasting tin (or similar size) and heat in the oven for 3–4 minutes until very hot.

3. Add the sausages, shallots and sage to the tin and heat through for a few minutes on the stove top to keep the oil really hot. Pour in the batter, pop into the oven straight away and bake for 25–30 minutes until golden and risen.

4. To make the gravy, whisk the granules into 200 ml boiling water until smooth and thickened, adding a little extra water if needed. Stir in the mustard and serve with the toad in the hole.

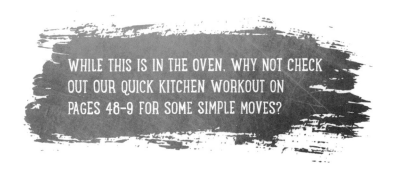

WHILE THIS IS IN THE OVEN, WHY NOT CHECK OUT OUR QUICK KITCHEN WORKOUT ON PAGES 48-9 FOR SOME SIMPLE MOVES?

chipotle pork
WITH CHIMICHURRI AND SLAW

SmartPoints values per serving 13
SmartPoints values per recipe 77

Preparation time 25 minutes
Cooking time 15 minutes
Serves 6

6 x 120 g trimmed pork loin steaks
1 tablespoon clear honey
100 g chipotle paste
300 g dried long grain rice
salt and freshly ground black pepper
lime wedges, to serve (optional)

For the chimichurri
a handful of fresh coriander,
    chopped finely
a handful of fresh parsley,
    chopped finely
1 garlic clove, crushed
1 small onion, chopped finely
2 tablespoons extra virgin olive oil
2 tablespoons red wine vinegar

For the slaw
1 red onion, sliced finely
½ white or green cabbage, sliced finely
1 tablespoon lime juice
150 g 0% fat natural yogurt
1 teaspoon toasted cumin seeds

Smoky chipotle and tangy chimichurri add a South American kick to this tasty dish.

1. Combine the ingredients for the chimichurri and season.

2. Combine the ingredients for the slaw and season with pepper.

3. Place the pork steaks in a shallow bowl, add the honey and chipotle paste and mix to coat. Preheat the grill and line the grill pan with foil. Grill the pork steaks for 12–15 minutes, turning once or twice.

4. Meanwhile, cook the rice according to the packet instructions and drain. Serve the rice with the chimichurri raked through, with a pork steak each and a heap of slaw. Serve with extra lime wedges, if using.

CLASSIC CHICKEN
cordon bleu

 SmartPoints values per serving 8
SmartPoints values per recipe 33

Preparation time 15 minutes
Cooking time 40 minutes
Serves 4

550 g white potatoes, cut into wedges
calorie controlled cooking spray
4 x 150 g skinless, boneless
    chicken breasts
100 g reduced fat soft cheese
50 g smoked ham, chopped
1 tablespoon snipped fresh chives
50 g dried breadcrumbs
1 tablespoon chopped fresh parsley
1 tablespoon plain flour
1 egg, beaten
16 cherry tomatoes on the vine
1 teaspoon olive oil
freshly ground black pepper

Breadcrumbed chicken parcels filled with soft cheese and ham, and served with wedges – perfect for a Friday night in.

1. Preheat the oven to Gas Mark 6/200°C/fan oven 180°C. Place the potato wedges on a baking tray and mist with the cooking spray. Mix well and season with freshly ground black pepper. Bake for 40 minutes, turning occasionally, until cooked through.

2. Meanwhile, sandwich the chicken breasts between two sheets of cling film, place on a board and bash with a rolling pin until about 3 cm thick. Mix together the soft cheese, ham and chives and spoon equal amounts of the mixture on to the chicken breasts. Fold over to make a parcel and press down to seal.

3. Mix the breadcrumbs with the parsley in a shallow dish. Place the flour and egg in separate shallow dishes and have a non-stick baking sheet to hand. Dip each chicken parcel first into the flour, then the egg and then the breadcrumbs, repeating the egg and breadcrumbs if the parcels are not fully coated. Place on the baking sheet, mist with cooking spray and bake alongside the wedges for 20–25 minutes, until golden and cooked through.

4. Meanwhile, put the tomatoes on another baking sheet, drizzle with the olive oil and roast for 10–15 minutes. Serve with the chicken parcels and potato wedges.

WITH TIME TO SPARE WHILE THIS DISH IS COOKING, CHECK OUT THE QUICK KITCHEN WORKOUT ON PAGES 48-9 FOR SOME SIMPLE MOVES.

roast chicken
WITH FAT OVEN CHIPS

SmartPoints values per serving 9
SmartPoints values per recipe 56

 Preparation time 20 minutes
Cooking time 1 hour 20 minutes
    + resting
Serves 6

1 lemon
1 x 1.5 kg chicken (900 g meat,
    skinless)
3 garlic cloves
calorie controlled cooking spray
800 g potatoes, scrubbed
2 tablespoons finely chopped fresh
    tarragon
80 g reduced fat mayonnaise
salt and freshly ground black pepper

Who doesn't love chicken and chips? Served with lemon-tarragon mayo and fresh veggies, this is an unbeatable meal.

1. Preheat the oven to Gas Mark 5/190°C/fan oven 170°C. Finely grate the zest from the lemon and set aside. Quarter the lemon.

2. Place the chicken in a large roasting tin and push the lemon quarters and garlic cloves into the body cavity. Season the chicken and mist with the cooking spray, rubbing the spray into the skin. Roast for 1 hour 20 minutes, or until cooked through (the juices should run clear when the thigh is pierced with a skewer).

3. Meanwhile, slice the potatoes into thick chips, keeping the skins on. Boil for 5 minutes, then drain and dry with kitchen paper. Place on a baking tray misted with cooking spray and mist the chips. Bake on a high shelf for 30–40 minutes, or until golden and cooked through.

4. Remove the chicken from the oven and wrap loosely in foil. Leave to rest in a warm place for 30 minutes before carving.

5. Stir the lemon zest and tarragon into the mayo. Divide the chips between 6 plates and serve with 150 g skinless roast chicken each, the mayo and cooked vegetables of your choice.

> **⚲ COOK'S TIP** Prefer your roast chicken with the skin on? The **SmartPoints** values will be 12 per serving.

chicken,
LEEK AND CIDER PIE

9 SmartPoints values per serving 9
SmartPoints values per recipe 36

Preparation time 30 minutes
Cooking time 30 minutes
Serves 4

1 teaspoon olive oil
1 leek, sliced
250 g mushrooms, sliced
450 g skinless chicken breast, cut
    into chunks
400 ml dry cider
1 chicken stock cube, crumbled
2 tablespoons half fat crème fraîche
750 g potatoes, peeled and sliced thinly
1 tablespoon low fat spread, melted
salt and freshly ground black pepper

Succulent chicken and zesty cider make a lovely combo in this moreish pie. Serve with steamed green vegetables of your choice.

1. Heat the oil in a large frying pan and, when hot, add the leek and mushrooms. Cook for 10 minutes over a low heat until softened. Remove from the pan and set aside. Reheat the pan, add the chicken and brown. Return the vegetables to the pan with the cider and stock cube. Bring to the boil, cover and simmer gently for 15 minutes, or until the chicken is cooked through. Remove from the heat and stir in the crème fraîche.

2. Meanwhile, bring a pan of water to the boil, add the potatoes, cover and boil for 5 minutes, or until just tender. Drain well and set aside.

3. Preheat the oven to Gas Mark 6/200°C/fan oven 180°C. Spoon the chicken mixture into a 2-litre baking dish. Arrange the potato slices over the top, brush with the melted spread and season. Bake for 25–30 minutes until golden.

GF To make this dish gluten free, simply replace the stock cube with a gluten free stock cube.

COOK'S TIP This dish can be prepared ahead: cook the filling and potatoes, assemble the pie, then cool and chill. When ready, bake for 45 minutes until piping hot and golden.

chicken AND SPRING VEGETABLE *stew*

 SmartPoints values per serving 4
SmartPoints values per recipe 16

Takes 1 hour 15 minutes
Serves 4

calorie controlled cooking spray
400 g skinless, boneless chicken
    breast, chopped
250 g leeks, trimmed and sliced
2 garlic cloves, crushed
250 g carrots, peeled and sliced
100 g pearl barley, rinsed
1.7 litres hot chicken stock, made
    with a cube
250 g cauliflower, broken into
    small florets
4 spring onions, sliced finely
150 g kale, sliced
salt and freshly ground black pepper

Pearl barley is wonderfully nutty and chewy, and is great added to soups and stews. It's a good source of fibre, too.

1. Mist a large saucepan with the cooking spray and place over a medium heat. Add the chicken and fry, stirring, for 5–8 minutes, or until browned. Remove from the pan and set aside.

2. Mist the pan again and add the leeks. Fry, stirring, for 5 minutes, or until starting to soften, adding a splash of water if they stick. Add the garlic and carrots and season. Fry, stirring, for 5 more minutes.

3. Return the chicken to the pan and stir in the pearl barley. Pour in 1.2 litres of the stock and cover. Bring to the boil and cook for 10 minutes, then reduce the heat and simmer for 30 minutes, or until the barley is tender.

4. Add the cauliflower to the stew with the remaining stock. Simmer, uncovered, for 10 minutes, adding the spring onions and kale for the final 3 minutes. Season to taste, then ladle into bowls and serve.

COOK'S TIP Soaking the pearl barley in cold water for 30 minutes while you prepare and cook the vegetables, then rinsing it in fresh cold water, will help it cook and give you a fluffier result.

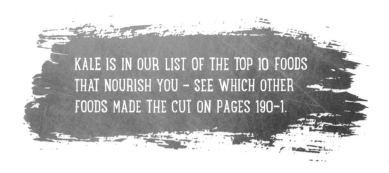

KALE IS IN OUR LIST OF THE TOP 10 FOODS THAT NOURISH YOU – SEE WHICH OTHER FOODS MADE THE CUT ON PAGES 190-1.

SWEET POTATO AND
turkey chilli

SmartPoints values per serving 5
SmartPoints values per recipe 32

Takes 45 minutes
Serves 6

calorie controlled cooking spray
500 g turkey breast mince
1 onion, chopped
2–3 garlic cloves, chopped
250 g sweet potatoes, cubed
1 teaspoon hot chilli powder
395 g can red kidney beans in
    chilli sauce
400 g can chopped tomatoes
2 large handfuls of spinach
salt and freshly ground black pepper

Turkey mince is low in fat and works really well in chilli in place of beef or pork.

1. Heat a wide non-stick sauté pan and mist with the cooking spray. Add the turkey, season and cook over a high heat for 5–6 minutes, breaking the mince up with a wooden spoon, until there is no pink meat left. Tip on to a plate and set aside.

2. Return the pan to the heat, mist again with cooking spray and add the onion, garlic and sweet potatoes with a splash of water. Cook over a medium-high heat for 15 minutes, stirring occasionally and adding more water if necessary to prevent sticking, until the vegetables are soft and lightly coloured.

3. Stir through the chilli powder, then add the kidney beans and tomatoes. Rinse the bean can, then fill it with water and add that plus the turkey. Simmer briskly for 15–20 minutes to reduce the liquid, then stir the spinach through until wilted. Serve straight away or pack into a lunchbox.

VARIATIONS Enjoy this spicy chilli with salad for a satisfying lunch, or turn it into a main meal with these extras for each person:
- 1 taco shell – 2 **SmartPoints** values
- 50 g dried brown rice – 5 **SmartPoints** values
- 25 g reduced fat Cheddar cheese, grated plus 1 tablespoon
    0% fat natural yogurt – 3 **SmartPoints** values

COOK'S TIP This will keep in the fridge for 2 days, or you can freeze it in individual portions for up to 1 month. Defrost thoroughly before reheating until piping hot.

BEAUTIFUL *salmon* WITH BEETROOT RÖSTI AND CUCUMBER SAUCE

SmartPoints values per serving 7
SmartPoints values per recipe 42

Takes 55 minutes
Serves 6

6 x 125 g salmon fillets
salt and freshly ground black pepper
lemon wedges, to serve
sprigs of fresh dill, roughly chopped,
    to garnish

For the sauce

½ cucumber, peeled, de-seeded and
    cubed finely
4 tablespoons half fat crème fraîche
2 tablespoons chopped fresh dill
1 teaspoon wholegrain mustard
1 tablespoon lemon juice

For the rösti

500 g Maris Piper potatoes
300 g raw beetroot, peeled and grated
4 spring onions, sliced
calorie controlled cooking spray

An impressive dish that's ideal for when you're entertaining friends and family.

1. To make the sauce, place the cucumber in a colander or nylon sieve, sprinkle with a little salt and allow to stand for 20 minutes. Place on a double layer of kitchen roll and squeeze out any excess moisture. Tip into a bowl and add the remaining ingredients. Season and chill until needed.

2. Meanwhile, peel and halve the potatoes for the rösti. Place in a saucepan of water, bring to the boil and boil rapidly for 5 minutes. Drain and cool a little. Grate the potatoes in a bowl, add the beetroot and spring onions and season well, then combine – it's easiest to do this with your hands so as not to break the potato up too much. Shape into 6 discs and set aside.

3. When you're ready, mist a large non-stick frying pan with the cooking spray and add the rösti (you'll need to do them in two batches). Cook for 10 minutes over a medium heat, turning occasionally. Once cooked, keep them warm in a low oven.

4. Preheat the grill and line the grill pan with foil. Season the salmon fillets and pop under the grill for 5–8 minutes until golden and flaking. To serve, place a fillet on top of a rösti, add a spoonful of the sauce and a lemon wedge, and garnish with dill.

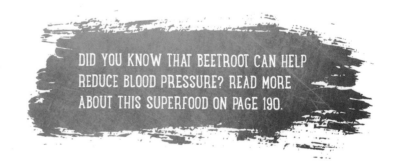

DID YOU KNOW THAT BEETROOT CAN HELP REDUCE BLOOD PRESSURE? READ MORE ABOUT THIS SUPERFOOD ON PAGE 190.

SIMPLE TUSCAN
fish stew

SmartPoints values per serving 6
SmartPoints values per recipe 22

Takes 35 minutes
Serves 4

2 teaspoons olive oil
1 small red onion, chopped finely
4 garlic cloves
2 tablespoons finely chopped fresh sage
2 tablespoons finely chopped fresh
    parsley, plus extra to garnish
1 teaspoon dried chilli flakes
2 tablespoons tomato purée
400 g can chopped tomatoes
850 ml fish stock, made with a cube
300 g skinless monkfish fillet, chopped
    into large chunks
250 g tilapia or pollock fillet, chopped
    into large chunks
150 g cooked shell-on king prawns
8 x 20 g slices ciabatta
lemon zest, to serve

Treat yourself to a taste of Tuscany with this zingy fish stew, served with toasted ciabatta to mop up the delicious broth.

1. Warm the oil in a large saucepan and add the onion, 3 of the garlic cloves, crushed, the herbs and the chilli flakes. Fry over a low heat, stirring, for 8 minutes, or until softened but not coloured. Add the tomato purée and cook, stirring, for a further 1 minute.

2. Add the tomatoes and fish stock and bring to the boil. Add the monkfish and simmer for 5 minutes. Add the tilapia and prawns and simmer for 5 minutes more, or until the fish is cooked through.

3. Meanwhile, toast the ciabatta slices and rub with the remaining peeled garlic clove. Ladle the stew into 4 bowls. Garnish with fresh parsley and lemon zest and serve with the toasted ciabatta.

THIS RECIPE USES LOTS OF STORECUPBOARD INGREDIENTS - CHECK OUT PAGES 12-13 FOR MORE ESSENTIALS.

FISH FINGER
wraps

7 SmartPoints values per serving 7
SmartPoints values per recipe 35

Preparation time 25 minutes
Cooking time 25 minutes
Serves 5

80 g (approx. 4 slices) calorie controlled
    white bread
1 tablespoon plain flour
1 egg, beaten
300 g skinless pollock fillets, sliced into
    finger-length strips
calorie controlled cooking spray
5 Weight Watchers wraps (or similar)
salt and freshly ground black pepper

For the sweetcorn salsa
198 g can sweetcorn, drained
½ small red onion, chopped finely
75 g cucumber, de-seeded and diced
1 red chilli, de-seeded and chopped
    finely (adjust to taste)
a small handful of fresh coriander
    leaves, chopped roughly
finely grated zest and juice of 1 lime

To serve
100 g red cabbage, shredded
100 g low fat natural yogurt
a pinch of paprika

A great twist on easy home-made fish fingers. You can assemble the wraps for everyone or let them dig in at the table – perfect for Saturday night feasting.

1. Make the salsa by combining the sweetcorn, onion, cucumber, chilli, coriander and lime zest and juice. Season and set aside. The salsa will keep, covered, in the fridge for 24 hours.

2. Preheat the oven to Gas Mark 4/180°C/fan oven 160°C. Blitz the bread in a food processor to make breadcrumbs and sprinkle them on a plate. Sprinkle the flour on a separate plate and pour the egg into a shallow bowl.

3. Dip the strips of pollock in the flour, then the egg and then the breadcrumbs. Arrange on a baking tray misted with the cooking spray and bake for 25 minutes, or until golden.

4. Meanwhile, grill the wraps for 2–3 minutes, or until browned and starting to crisp up. Top with a handful of red cabbage, the sweetcorn salsa, the fish fingers, a spoonful of yogurt and a pinch of paprika. The wraps can either be served open (grill them for a few minutes more to ensure they are extra crispy) or folded up.

mini
LENTIL PIES

 SmartPoints values per serving 6
SmartPoints values per recipe 37

 Preparation time 40 minutes
Cooking time 45 minutes
Serves 6

calorie controlled cooking spray
1 red onion, chopped
2 celery sticks, chopped
1 large courgette, chopped
1 large red pepper, de-seeded
    and chopped
3 garlic cloves, chopped
60 g dried red lentils
½ tablespoon medium curry powder
2 x 400 g cans chopped tomatoes
½ vegetable stock cube
300 ml boiling water
390 g can green lentils, drained
1 kg floury potatoes, peeled and
    chopped
40 g low fat spread
salt and freshly ground black pepper
Tabasco sauce, to serve (optional)

Great served with a steamed green vegetable such as broccoli or with a green salad.

1. Heat a heavy based saucepan and mist with the cooking spray. Add the onion and celery and cook briskly for 5 minutes, or until starting to soften. Add the courgette, pepper and garlic and cook for another 5 minutes, then stir in the red lentils and curry powder and cook for 1 minute before adding the tomatoes, crumbled stock cube and boiling water.

2. Bring to the boil for 10 minutes, then reduce the heat and simmer for 15 minutes, or until reduced but still juicy. Add a little hot water if it looks too dry. Stir in the green lentils and season to taste.

3. Meanwhile, preheat the oven to Gas Mark 5/190ºC/fan oven 170ºC. Boil the potatoes until tender, then drain well and mash with 30 g of the low fat spread.

4. Divide the lentil mixture between 6 ovenproof dishes (or use 1 large dish) and top with the mashed potato. Dot with the remaining low fat spread and cook for 45 minutes, or until golden on top and piping hot. Serve with a dash of Tabasco, if you like.

COOK'S TIP For an extra treat, top the mashed potato with 100 g grated half fat Cheddar cheese before baking. This will give the meal a **SmartPoints** value of 8 per serving.

IF YOU HAVE TIME TO SPARE WHILE THIS IS COOKING, WHY NOT CHECK OUT THE QUICK KITCHEN WORKOUT ON PAGES 48-9 FOR SOME SIMPLE MOVES?

THREE CHEESE *cannelloni*

SmartPoints values per serving 9
SmartPoints values per recipe 36

Preparation time 20 minutes
Cooking time 50 minutes
Serves 4

2 teaspoons olive oil
1 aubergine, cut into 1 cm cubes
1 red pepper, de-seeded and cut into
    1 cm cubes
1 large courgette, cut into 1 cm cubes
3 garlic cloves, chopped
500 g carton passata
1 teaspoon sugar
8 cannelloni tubes
125 g pack light mozzarella, sliced
salt and freshly ground black pepper

For the filling
25 g sun-dried tomatoes
150 g ricotta cheese
50 g grated vegetarian Italian hard
    cheese
a handful of fresh basil, chopped, plus
    a few whole leaves to garnish

A rich and satisfying veggie meal that the family will adore. Serve with garlic bread and a large rocket salad for an extra 4 SmartPoints values per serving.

1. Place the sun-dried tomatoes in a small bowl and cover with boiling water. Set aside to soak for 10 minutes then drain (reserving the liquid) and chop. Top up the reserved liquid to 200 ml with water.

2. Meanwhile, heat the oil in a large frying pan and add the aubergine and a little seasoning. Fry over a medium-high heat for 5 minutes, adding a splash of water if it sticks, then add the pepper, courgette and garlic. Cook for a further 5 minutes then add the passata, sugar and reserved soaking liquid. Bring to the boil then season to taste.

3. Combine the ricotta, sun-dried tomatoes, grated hard cheese and basil, and season. Push this mixture into the cannelloni tubes using your fingers or a piping bag.

4. Preheat the oven to Gas Mark 5/190°C/fan oven 170°C. Pour about one-third of the passata mixture into a small lasagne dish, then lay the stuffed cannelloni tubes on top. Spoon over the remaining sauce, top with the mozzarella and bake for 45–50 minutes, or until golden and bubbling. Cover with foil halfway through if it starts to brown too much.

5. Let the dish sit for 5–10 minutes then scatter with the reserved basil leaves and serve.

COOK'S TIP To make short work of filling the cannelloni tubes, spoon the filling into a plastic food bag and snip off the corner. Voilà – an instant piping bag!

To freeze, cool the dish completely once cooked, cover with foil, pop into a freezer bag and freeze for up to 1 month. Defrost thoroughly and warm through in the oven, keeping the foil over the top.

Leftover ricotta cheese? Spread 25 g on a Ryvita crispbread and top with 3 jumbo prawns for a **SmartPoints** value of 2.

AFRICAN *vegetable* STEW WITH SWEET POTATOES AND PEANUTS

9 SmartPoints values per serving 9
SmartPoints values per recipe 37

GF Takes 30 minutes
Serves 4

V

2 teaspoons sunflower oil
1 large red onion, chopped roughly
2 celery sticks, chopped
2 carrots, chopped
3 garlic cloves, chopped
2 peppers, de-seeded and chopped
(we used red and green)
500 g sweet potatoes, peeled and cut
into 3 cm chunks
400 g butternut squash, cut into
small wedges
2 tablespoons Baharat spice mix
50 g jumbo salted peanuts, rinsed
with hot water
1 green chilli, chopped finely, plus
extra to serve (optional)
500 ml hot vegetable stock
(see page 220)
50 g reduced fat peanut butter
a handful of fresh coriander, chopped

Peanuts feature widely in African cuisine and add an intense flavour dimension to this one-pot veggie meal. You could serve this stew with a naan bread. A Weight Watchers mini plain naan is 3 extra SmartPoints.

1. Heat the oil in a large saucepan. Add the onion, celery and carrots, and cook for 5 minutes on a medium heat. Add the garlic, peppers, sweet potatoes and squash, and cook for 5 minutes, stirring. Add the spice mix, peanuts and chilli and cook for 1 minute until fragrant. Add the stock, bring to the boil, cover and simmer gently for 12–15 minutes until all the vegetables are just tender.

2. Put about 6 tablespoons of cooking liquor in a small bowl and mix with the peanut butter, then stir gently into the stew and simmer for 1 minute to thicken slightly. Scatter with coriander and serve with extra chopped chilli, if you like.

> **🍴 COOK'S TIPS** If you cannot find Baharat spice mix, you can use 2 teaspoons paprika, 2 teaspoons ground coriander and 1 teaspoon ground mixed spice instead.
>
> You can reheat uneaten portions the next day or freeze in freezerproof containers for up to 1 month. Reheat until piping hot, then garnish with fresh coriander and chilli.

THIS RECIPE USES LOTS OF STORECUPBOARD INGREDIENTS – CHECK OUT PAGES 12–13 FOR MORE ESSENTIALS.

Happy people
MAKE
HEALTHIER CHOICES

Losing weight is only part of the journey to becoming your best self. Taking care of yourself and realising your self-worth away from the scales is a huge part of feeling content and happy in life. So while food and your body health is important, it's also essential to take care of yourself in other ways.

So check out these 'happiness skills' to help you feel better from the inside out – after all, happy people make healthier choices!

positivity

A positive attitude not only improves your mood, but can make your weight-loss journey a little less overwhelming, too. Surround yourself with positive energy: celebrate your weight losses so far; create a personal mood board with motivational quotes and pictures; or meet up with a friend who's a positive influence in your life.

mindfulness

Being more mindful will help you to be more aware of yourself – and it's also been shown to help decrease stress, anxiety, and help improve sleep. Try de-cluttering your mind by spending five minutes sitting quietly with eyes closed and taking a few deep breaths while letting your mind slow down. It will help you refocus and feel more motivated.

mindful eating

Like mindfulness in general, mindful eating helps you to be aware of what you're eating – and helps you to enjoy it more! Take time to really savour your food: turn off the TV, chew more slowly, and enjoy the flavours and textures. By taking more time to appreciate food, you're less likely to eat mindlessly when you're bored or stressed.

gratitude

Taking time to feel grateful for the good things in your life can help you feel more optimistic – which can only be a good thing when on the journey! Take a few minutes every day to make a note of three things you're grateful for – it can be as small as enjoying your lunch break or as big as going on holiday – and look back on your list when you're in need of an optimism boost.

strengths

We all have individual character strengths. Take time to appreciate yours and flex your personality 'muscles': if you're creative, try a new artistic skill; if you're a leader, try organising a group activity; if you're curious, pick up a new book. Using your strengths helps improve your self-esteem and boosts your energy.

hope

Feeling hopeful is a big part of feeling happier – people who have higher hopes are not only more optimistic, but they're usually more successful. Keep your hopes in high spirits by breaking your big goals into smaller ones. The more small goals you achieve, the more hopeful you'll feel about reaching the big one – and the closer you'll be to getting there!

smoothies, juices and soups

BLUEBERRY *soy smoothie*

 SmartPoints values per serving 5
SmartPoints values per recipe 10

 Takes 5 minutes
Serves 2

1 small ripe banana, chopped
175 g blueberries (reserve a few for decoration)
350 ml light soya milk

Banana and blueberries combine beautifully in this satisfying milk-free smoothie.

1. Place all the ingredients in a blender and whizz until smooth. Pour into 2 tall glasses and serve topped with the reserved berries.

> **COOK'S TIP** This smoothie is best served straightaway, as the banana starts to discolour and thicken soon after blending.

MANGO AND PISTACHIO *lassi*

 SmartPoints values per serving 6
SmartPoints values per recipe 12

 Takes 5 minutes
Serves 2

1 ripe mango, stoned and peeled
50 g 0% fat natural Greek yogurt
200 ml skimmed milk
15 g pistachio nuts, chopped finely

A smooth, refreshing yogurt drink originating in India.

1. Place the mango, yogurt and milk in a blender and whizz until smooth. Pour into 2 glasses and scatter with the chopped pistachios. Serve immediately.

> **COOK'S TIP** Store all the ingredients, including the mango, in the fridge until you need them, to make sure your lassi is perfectly chilled without the need for ice.

home-made
LEMONADE WITH MINT

2 SmartPoints values per serving 2
SmartPoints values per recipe 10

GF Takes 15 minutes + chilling
Serves 6

V

peeled rind of 6 unwaxed lemons plus
    300 ml lemon juice
a handful of fresh mint, leaves stripped
30 g agave nectar
sprigs of fresh mint, to decorate
    (optional)
lemon slices, to serve

A thirst-quenching fresh lemon drink ideal for warm summer days.

1. Put the lemon rind, mint leaves, agave nectar and 300 ml water in a saucepan and bring to the boil, stirring until the sweetener has dissolved. Simmer for 5 minutes, then remove from the heat and leave to cool completely.

2. Strain into a jug, flask or bottle, add the lemon juice and 1.2 litres water. Chill until ready to use. Serve cold with lemon slices and decorated with mint sprigs, if you like.

REALLY FRESH spiced
CELERY JUICE

4 SmartPoints per serving 4
SmartPoints values per recipe 4

GF Takes 5 minutes
Serves 1

V

1 pear, de-seeded
2 celery sticks, plus extra to garnish
2 handfuls of chopped kale
a small handful of fresh parsley
a pinch of turmeric

Celery adds a great savoury flavour to drinks as well as providing lots of juice.

1. Place the pear, celery, kale and parsley in a juicer and blend. Add a couple of tablespoons of cold water to the machine to rinse through and thin the juice. Season with a pinch of turmeric and garnish with a celery stick.

CREAMY COCONUT AND

avocado

5 SmartPoints value™ | **SmartPoints** values per serving 5
SmartPoints values per recipe 10

GF | **Takes 5 minutes**
Serves 2

V

½ avocado, peeled and stoned
2 handfuls of spinach
400 ml coconut water

A super-speedy juice that is sure to fill you up.

1. Place the avocado and spinach in a tall jug and use a hand-held blender to blend until smooth. Add the coconut water a little at a time, blending continuously until you have a smooth drink. Serve the drink immediately.

 *rhubarb* AND PEAR
WITH GINGER AND HONEY

6 SmartPoints value™ | **SmartPoints** values per serving 6
SmartPoints values per recipe 12

GF | **Takes 10 minutes + cooling**
Serves 2

V

300 g rhubarb, trimmed and chopped
2 pears, de-seeded
a small piece of fresh root ginger,
    peeled
2 teaspoons honey

The rhubarb gives this drink a lovely pink hue. If you like a long drink, dilute it with sparkling water.

1. Place the rhubarb in a small pan with 2 tablespoons water, bring to the boil, cover and simmer for around 5 minutes until completely broken down. Cool slightly then push through a fine sieve or muslin to extract the juice, then cool completely.

2. Juice the pears with the ginger and stir in the honey. Add as much of the strained rhubarb juice as you like – it's quite tart, so add a little and taste before adding more.

> **🍴 COOK'S TIP** 300 g rhubarb makes around 150 ml rhubarb juice, which will keep covered in the fridge for 2–3 days or can be frozen for later.

curried
PARSNIP SOUP

SmartPoints values per serving 7
SmartPoints values per recipe 26

 Takes 40 minutes
Serves 4

1 onion, chopped finely
2 celery sticks, chopped finely
700 g parsnips, peeled and chopped
    finely
2 garlic cloves, chopped finely
½ teaspoon turmeric
20 g fresh root ginger, peeled and
    chopped finely
2 teaspoons garam masala
1.25 litres hot vegetable stock (see page
    220)
40 g root vegetable crisps
salt and freshly ground black pepper
chopped fresh coriander, to serve

A velvety smooth soup that is deliciously warming – especially good when it's cold outside. Without the veg crisps it's 5 SmartPoints values per serving and a No Count recipe.

1. Place a large lidded saucepan over a low heat. Add the onion, celery and parsnips with 5 tablespoons water and season. Cover with a piece of greaseproof paper and the pan lid and sweat for 20 minutes, stirring occasionally so that the vegetables don't stick (add a splash more water if necessary).

2. Stir in the garlic, turmeric, ginger and garam masala. Re-cover with the greaseproof paper and lid and sweat for a further 5 minutes, or until the vegetables have softened.

3. Discard the greaseproof paper. Pour in the hot stock, cover and bring to the boil. Reduce the heat and simmer for 10 minutes. Ladle the soup into a blender – you may need to do this in batches – and blitz until smooth. Season to taste.

4. Ladle the soup into 4 warmed serving bowls. Scatter each bowl with 10 g vegetable crisps and some fresh coriander, and serve.

THIS RECIPE USES LOTS OF STORECUPBOARD INGREDIENTS – CHECK OUT PAGES 12–13 FOR MORE ESSENTIALS.

DELICIOUS *watercress* AND ROASTED GARLIC SOUP

SmartPoints values per serving 3
SmartPoints values per recipe 10

Takes 40 minutes
Serves 4

6 garlic cloves, plus extra to garnish
  (optional)
calorie controlled cooking spray
a bunch of spring onions, chopped,
  plus extra to garnish
1 leek, trimmed, washed and chopped
2–3 potatoes, peeled and chopped
  roughly (about 430 g peeled weight)
1.2 litres vegetable stock (see page
  220)
150 g watercress, reserving a few leaves
  for garnish
salt and freshly ground black pepper

Peppery watercress packs a flavour punch and makes great salads, sauces and soups.

1. Preheat the oven to Gas Mark 6/200°C/fan oven 180°C. Place the garlic cloves, still in their papery skins, on a baking tray and roast for 20–25 minutes until soft.

2. Heat a large deep saucepan and spray with the cooking spray. Sauté the spring onions and leek for 4–5 minutes until starting to soften.

3. Add the potatoes, stock and some coarsely ground black pepper, and simmer for 15–20 minutes until the potato is tender.

4. When the garlic is ready, squeeze the roasted cloves from their papery skins and add to the soup, together with the watercress. Cook for a further 2–3 minutes until the watercress has wilted.

5. Remove from the heat and blend to your desired consistency (we kept ours quite chunky), either with a hand-held blender or in a food processor. Season to taste and serve, garnished with shredded spring onions, watercress leaves and more roasted garlic cloves, if you like.

super-smooth
CELERIAC AND FENNEL SOUP

 4 SmartPoints value™

SmartPoints values per serving 4
SmartPoints values per recipe 8

 GF Takes 35 minutes
Serves 2

 V

calorie controlled cooking spray
1 onion, sliced
1 garlic clove, sliced
500 ml vegetable stock (see page 220)
½ celeriac, cubed
100 g potato, cubed
300 ml skimmed milk
½ fennel bulb, sliced (reserve a few
    fronds for garnish)
juice of 1 lemon
a pinch of nutmeg
2 tablespoons reduced fat crème
    fraîche
salt and freshly ground black pepper

The fennel gives this creamy soup a wonderful hint of aniseed – but you can simply leave it out if you prefer.

1. Mist a saucepan with the cooking spray and soften the onion and garlic for a few minutes. Add the stock to the pan, along with the celeriac, potato and milk.

2. Bring to the boil and simmer until tender, then add the fennel and warm through.

3. Using a blender, purée the soup, add the lemon juice and nutmeg, and season to taste.

4. Divide between 2 warmed bowls or mugs, stir in the crème fraîche and garnish with the fennel fronds.

> **COOK'S TIP** If you double up the recipe, this soup can be frozen in portions for up to 3 months.

hearty LENTIL AND VEGETABLE soup

SmartPoints values per serving 2
SmartPoints values per recipe 14

GF
Takes 30 minutes
Serves 6

V

calorie controlled cooking spray
1 onion, cubed finely
1 celery heart, trimmed and sliced finely
1 large carrot, sliced finely
1 large courgette, cubed finely
2 garlic cloves, crushed
1 tablespoon tomato purée
1 teaspoon dried thyme
75 ml white wine
2 x 200 g cans *chair de tomate*
    (see Cook's tip)
700 ml vegetable or chicken stock,
    made with 1½ cubes
15 g dried wild mushrooms
2 x 400 g cans Puy lentils in water,
    drained and rinsed
a few fresh parsley leaves

This chunky soup, thickened with nutty-tasting Puy lentils, is a meal on its own.

1. Heat a large, lidded, non-stick saucepan and mist with the cooking spray. Cook the onion, celery, carrot, courgette and garlic, covered, for 5–6 minutes until softened. Stir in the tomato purée and dried thyme and cook for 1 minute.

2. Add the wine and *chair de tomate* and cook for 1–2 minutes. Pour in the stock, add the mushrooms and bring to the boil. Continue to simmer for 10 minutes until the vegetables are tender and the soup has thickened slightly.

3. Add the lentils and heat until warmed through. Sprinkle with the parsley and serve.

COOK'S TIP *Chair de tomate* is finely chopped tomatoes in a rich tomato sauce, available in cans in larger supermarkets. You can use normal chopped tomatoes if you prefer.

SPICY SWEET POTATO AND
coconut soup

SmartPoints values per serving 7
SmartPoints values per recipe 26

Takes 40 minutes
Serves 4

calorie controlled cooking spray
1 leek, chopped
2 teaspoons garam masala
450 g sweet potatoes, peeled and
    cubed
1 small butternut squash, peeled,
    de-seeded and cubed
700 ml vegetable or chicken stock,
    made with 1½ cubes
15 g creamed coconut
2 teaspoons harissa
4 tablespoons low fat natural yogurt
salt and freshly ground black pepper
a few fresh chives, snipped, to garnish

An exotic-tasting full-bodied soup.

1. Heat a large non-stick saucepan and mist with the cooking spray. Cook the leek for 3–4 minutes until softened but not browned. Add the garam masala and cook for 30 seconds.

2. Add the sweet potatoes, butternut squash and stock and bring to the boil. Simmer for 15–20 minutes until the vegetables are tender. Stir in the creamed coconut and whizz in a blender until the soup is smooth.

3. Return to the pan and gently reheat if necessary, then check the seasoning and ladle into bowls. Swirl each bowl with ½ teaspoon harissa and 1 tablespoon yogurt, then sprinkle with a few chives.

> **COOK'S TIP** If you fancy having a go at making your own harissa paste, there's a quick and easy recipe on page 216.

shredded VEGETABLE AND BAMBOO SHOOT CLEAR SOUP

SmartPoints values per serving 0
SmartPoints values per recipe 1

Takes 30 minutes
Serves 4

GF

V

850 ml vegetable stock (see page 220)
½ teaspoon Chinese five spice
1 large carrot, julienned
a bunch of spring onions, sliced finely
150 g mangetout or sugar snap peas,
    sliced finely
225 g can bamboo shoots, drained and
    sliced
2 teaspoons finely grated fresh
    root ginger
1 small red chilli, sliced finely
salt and freshly ground black pepper
a few sprigs of fresh coriander, to
    garnish

A Chinese-inspired clear soup full of vegetable goodness.

1. Heat the vegetable stock and Chinese five spice in a large saucepan until boiling. Add all the remaining ingredients apart from the coriander and return to the boil.

2. Reduce the heat and simmer for 8–10 minutes. Taste and season if needed. Ladle the soup into warmed bowls and serve garnished with a sprig of coriander.

> **COOK'S TIP** To save time, use ready-prepared fresh or frozen stir-fry vegetables instead of the carrot, spring onions and mangetout or sugar snap peas.

butternut
AND CORIANDER SOUP

SmartPoints values per serving 2
SmartPoints values per recipe 9

Takes 40 minutes
Serves 4

calorie controlled cooking spray
1 onion, chopped
1 garlic clove, crushed
1 celery stick, chopped
1 carrot, peeled and chopped
1 kg butternut squash, peeled,
    de-seeded and cut into chunks
850 ml vegetable stock (see page 220)
40 g pumpkin seeds
1 tablespoon soy sauce
2 teaspoons ground coriander
juice of ½ lemon
salt and freshly ground black pepper
fresh coriander leaves, chopped,
    to serve

A comforting bowl of creamy-tasting soup to chase away the autumn chill.

1. Mist a large saucepan with the cooking spray. Add the onion, garlic, celery and carrot and cook over a low heat until soft but not coloured. Add the squash and vegetable stock and bring to a simmer. Leave to cook until all the vegetables are soft, about 20 minutes.

2. Meanwhile, mix the pumpkin seeds with the soy sauce and toast the seeds in a small dry frying pan for a few minutes, tossing the pan every 20 seconds or so. Tip out on to greaseproof paper and leave to dry.

3. Transfer the soup to a food processor or use a hand-held blender to blitz until smooth. Return to the pan and add the ground coriander and lemon juice. Heat through and season to taste. Divide between 4 warmed bowls and serve topped with the toasted pumpkin seeds and fresh coriander leaves.

COOK'S TIP Fancy a chunkier soup? Blend only half the vegetables and return them to the pan with the whole ones. If you have any soup left over, try adding some zero **SmartPoints** values vegetables to turn it into a filling stew.

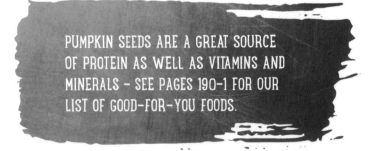

PUMPKIN SEEDS ARE A GREAT SOURCE OF PROTEIN AS WELL AS VITAMINS AND MINERALS – SEE PAGES 190-1 FOR OUR LIST OF GOOD-FOR-YOU FOODS.

spinach AND POTATO SOUP WITH PESTO AND POACHED EGG

6

SmartPoints values per serving 6
SmartPoints values per recipe 24

Preparation time 10 minutes
Cooking time 35 minutes
Serves 4

1 teaspoon olive oil
1 large onion, chopped
2 garlic cloves, chopped
500 g peeled potatoes, cut into
   bite-size chunks
1 litre vegetable stock (see page 220)
200 g bag spinach

To serve
4 very fresh eggs
4 teaspoons good quality pesto
   (see Cook's tip)

Spinach is a powerhouse vegetable that is also delicious eaten raw in salads.

1. Heat a large, heavy based saucepan and add the olive oil. Cook the onion for about 15 minutes until softened and translucent, adding splashes of water as you go to stop it from sticking.

2. Add the garlic and potatoes and cook for another 2 minutes, stirring, then add the stock. Bring to the boil then simmer for 15–20 minutes, or until the potatoes are tender.

3. Stir in the spinach and let it wilt down, then take about half of the mixture and blend it until smooth. Return the blended mixture to the pan and keep the soup warm.

4. Meanwhile, poach the eggs in a pan of simmering water, then drain on kitchen paper.

5. Divide the soup between 4 warmed bowls and top with a poached egg and 1 teaspoon of pesto each. Serve immediately.

 To make this No Count, just leave out the pesto when serving.

> **COOK'S TIP** Many pestos aren't vegetarian, so be sure to check the label.

CHILLI, CARROT AND SPINACH
soup

 SmartPoints values per serving 1
SmartPoints values per recipe 2

Takes 45 minutes
Serves 4

calorie controlled cooking spray
1 onion, chopped
1 celery stick, chopped
1 garlic clove, sliced
450 g carrots, chopped
1 litre hot vegetable stock (see page 220)
½ teaspoon dried chilli flakes
25 g fresh coriander, leaves and stalks separated
25 g baby spinach
1 tablespoon half fat crème fraîche
½ red chilli, sliced
salt and freshly ground black pepper

The chilli adds a lovely spicy kick to this fresh-tasting vegetable soup.

1. Heat a large saucepan and mist with the cooking spray, then add the onion and celery and cook until soft and translucent. Add the garlic and cook for a further minute.

2. Next add the carrots and stock, followed by the dried chilli flakes and coriander stalks. Bring to the boil then simmer for 30 minutes.

3. Put the soup in a food processor or use a hand-held blender and blitz until smooth. Return to the pan and season well. Add the spinach (it will wilt in the heat of the pan). Stir in the crème fraîche and serve sprinkled with slices of red chilli and the coriander leaves, if you like.

For a No Count version, simply leave out the half fat crème fraîche

COOK'S TIP If freezing, add the spinach and crème fraîche later, once defrosted.

sweetcorn, CHILLI AND CORIANDER *soup*

SmartPoints values per serving 5
SmartPoints values per recipe 21

Takes 30 minutes
Serves 4

calorie controlled cooking spray
1 onion, chopped roughly
1 red chilli, cubed finely (reserve a few
    cubes to garnish)
900 ml vegetable stock (see page 220)
175 g cauliflower, chopped into
    small florets
600 g frozen sweetcorn, defrosted
a handful of fresh coriander, plus extra
    to garnish
salt and freshly ground black pepper

Who needs the Chinese takeaway when you can whizz up this fabulous thick chowder in half an hour?

1. Heat a large non-stick saucepan and mist with the cooking spray. Cook the onion and chilli for 3–4 minutes, or until it begins to soften. Add the stock and bring to the boil. Add the cauliflower and simmer for 3 minutes, then add half the sweetcorn and bring back to a simmer. Cook for 2 minutes, or until just tender.

2. Add the coriander and whizz in a blender until smooth and creamy. Return the soup to the pan, stir in the remaining sweetcorn and season to taste. Keep warm or reheat if necessary. Ladle into bowls and serve immediately, topped with the reserved chilli and coriander.

🍴 COOK'S TIP This soup freezes well. Cool thoroughly and freeze for up to 1 month.

HEARTY GOLDEN
vegetable soup

SmartPoints values per serving 7
SmartPoints values per recipe 28

Takes 40 minutes
Serves 4

GF

V

calorie controlled cooking spray
2 onions, chopped
2 garlic cloves, crushed
600 g sweet potatoes, scrubbed and
    chopped roughly
1 butternut squash, or 1 small to
    medium pumpkin, peeled,
    de-seeded and chopped roughly
100 g red lentils
a pinch of dried chilli flakes, plus extra
    to garnish
1.2 litres vegetable stock (see page
    220)
red or green chillies, sliced finely, to
    garnish
salt and freshly ground black pepper

A handful of lentils will thicken soup to make it extra satisfying, as well as providing valuable protein.

1. Mist a large lidded saucepan with the cooking spray, then gently stir-fry the onions and garlic with 4 tablespoons water until softened but not brown.

2. Add the sweet potatoes and squash or pumpkin, along with the lentils, chilli flakes and stock. Cover and bring to the boil. (Add extra stock if you prefer a thinner soup.)

3. Turn down the heat and simmer for 20 minutes, or until the vegetables are tender. Cool briefly, then whizz in a blender to make a thick, smooth soup. Reheat if necessary, then season to taste and serve sprinkled with sliced fresh chilli and dried chilli flakes.

VARIATION If you prefer, you can use potatoes instead of sweet potatoes and carrots instead of butternut squash or pumpkin. The **SmartPoints** values per serving will remain the same.

> **🍴 COOK'S TIP** If you don't like your food too hot then you can simply leave out the chillies.

SPRING
minestrone

6 SmartPoints value™

SmartPoints values per serving 6
SmartPoints values per recipe 23

Takes 20 minutes
Serves 4

calorie controlled cooking spray
1 large carrot, diced
70 g pancetta cubes
1 litre vegetable stock, made with
    a cube
100 g conchigliette pasta
2 spring onions, sliced
110 g trimmed Tenderstem broccoli
110 g fine green beans, halved
100 g asparagus tips, halved
fresh basil leaves, to garnish (optional)
4 heaped teaspoons pesto, to serve

With its vegetable medley and tiny pasta shells, this speedy soup pays homage to the Italian favourite.

1. Heat a heavy based saucepan, mist with the cooking spray and add the carrot and pancetta. Sauté, stirring, for 5 minutes, or until golden.

2. Add the stock and bring to the boil, then add the pasta. Simmer for 5 minutes, then add the vegetables and cook for another 3–4 minutes, or until the pasta and vegetables are just tender.

3. Divide between 4 warmed bowls, garnish with a few basil leaves, if using, and serve with a spoonful of pesto.

V **VARIATION** Omit the pancetta and use vegetarian pesto. Sauté the carrots in 2 teaspoons olive oil, along with a small sliced leek. The soup will have a **SmartPoints** value of 6 per serving.

> 🍴 **COOK'S TIP** If you want to make a meal of it, try serving this soup with 40 g warm granary bread, for an extra 3 **SmartPoints** values per serving, or 30 g medium fat goat's cheese, also for an extra 3 **SmartPoints** values per serving.

BROCCOLI IS GREAT FOR HELPING TO KEEP EYES, HAIR AND NAILS HEALTHY – SEE PAGES 190–1 FOR MORE NOURISHING FOODS.

BEEF *pho*

SmartPoints values per serving 5
SmartPoints values per recipe 9

GF

Takes 15 minutes
Serves 2

850 ml hot beef stock, made with
    1½ cubes
a small piece of fresh root ginger,
    peeled and sliced
75 g bean sprouts
2 spring onions, sliced
1 small red chilli, de-seeded and
    sliced thinly
100 g ready to serve rice noodles
1 tablespoon Thai fish sauce
175 g sirloin steak, trimmed of fat and
    sliced as thinly as possible
1 small head pak choi, sliced
a small handful of fresh basil leaves,
    torn roughly, to garnish (optional)
lime wedges, to serve (optional)

Pho is a Vietnamese noodle soup. This version is quick to prepare, and looks and tastes stunning.

1. Heat the beef stock and ginger in a large saucepan until boiling. Add the bean sprouts, spring onions, chilli, noodles and fish sauce and return to the boil.

2. Reduce the heat, then add the steak and pak choi. Simmer for 1–2 minutes until the steak is just cooked. Divide the pho between 2 warmed bowls, scatter the basil over and serve with the lime wedges, if liked.

> **COOK'S TIP** In a hurry? Make this soup even more speedy by using 200 g ready-prepared mixed veg. The **SmartPoints** values will be the same.

classic
PEA AND HAM SOUP

5 SmartPoints value

SmartPoints values per serving 5
SmartPoints values per recipe 20

Takes 30 minutes
Serves 4

2 teaspoons sunflower oil
1 leek, chopped finely
1 garlic clove, chopped
250 g floury potatoes, peeled and cubed
1 litre hot weak vegetable stock (see page 220)
250 g frozen peas
200 g thick cut premium ham, chopped roughly
4 tablespoons very low fat natural fromage frais
salt and freshly ground black pepper

An all-time classic soup – comfort in a bowl.

1. Heat the oil in a large saucepan, add the leek and cook for 5 minutes until softened. Add the garlic and potatoes and cook for 2 minutes, stirring all the time. Add the stock, bring to the boil and simmer for 5 minutes, or until the potatoes are tender.

2. Add the peas, bring back to the boil and simmer for 5 minutes. Whizz the soup with a hand-held blender, leaving a little bit of texture if you like. Stir the ham into the soup and simmer until hot. Check the seasoning, then serve with a tablespoonful of fromage frais.

> **COOK'S TIP** This soup would taste gorgeous with some garlicky bruschetta with goat's cheese. Griddle a 40 g piece of French bread cut on the diagonal. Drizzle with ½ teaspoon olive oil and rub with a cut garlic clove. Top with 25 g soft goat's cheese for an extra **SmartPoints** value of 6 per serving.
>
> Don't be tempted to season the soup before you've tasted it as the ham and stock can be quite salty.

under
30
minutes

plaice
WITH PEAS, LETTUCE AND PANCETTA

 SmartPoints values per serving 11
SmartPoints values per recipe 22

 Takes 25 minutes
Serves 2

6 pearl onions or small shallots
70 g pancetta cubes
2 small Little Gem lettuces, quartered
100 ml chicken stock, made with
    ¼ cube
150 g fresh or frozen peas
2 tablespoons half fat crème fraîche
a handful of chopped fresh tarragon,
    chives or parsley
2 x 220 g plaice fillets
1 teaspoon low fat spread
salt and freshly ground black pepper

Plaice is a flatfish so takes very little time to cook – ideal for a quick midweek supper.

1. Cut the tops off the pearl onions or shallots and place them in a heatproof bowl. Cover with boiling water and leave for 5 minutes, then drain and cool a little before peeling off their skins. Halve.

2. Put the pancetta and onions in a large non-stick frying pan and heat gently until the pancetta begins to release some of its fat. Cook gently until the pancetta is just crisp and the onions are softened and golden.

3. Add the lettuce quarters and sauté for 1–2 minutes, then add the stock. Cook for another 1–2 minutes, then stir in the peas and cook until the peas are just tender.

4. Stir in the crème fraîche and herbs and season to taste. Meanwhile, heat a grill and line the grill pan with foil. Lay the plaice fillets on skin-side down, dot with the spread and season. Grill for 4–5 minutes until just cooked. Serve with the peas, lettuce and pancetta.

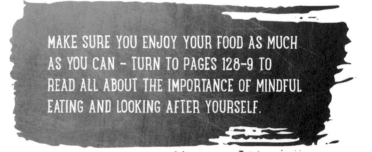

MAKE SURE YOU ENJOY YOUR FOOD AS MUCH AS YOU CAN – TURN TO PAGES 128-9 TO READ ALL ABOUT THE IMPORTANCE OF MINDFUL EATING AND LOOKING AFTER YOURSELF.

SPEEDY GARLIC, CHILLI AND
coriander prawns

3 SmartPoints values per serving 3
SmartPoints value™ SmartPoints values per recipe 22

Takes 15 minutes
Serves 8 (as part of a mixed tapas)

GF

5 fat garlic cloves, grated
½–¾ red chilli, chopped finely
a large handful of finely chopped
    fresh coriander leaves and stalks
50 g unsalted butter, softened
600 g raw tiger prawns, shelled but tail
    left on, de-veined
salt and freshly ground black pepper
1 lemon, plus lemon wedges to serve

Prawns make everything taste good, as do garlic, chilli and butter, so this dish is clearly going to be a winner all round.

1. Mash the garlic, chilli and coriander into the butter.

2. Heat a sauté pan. Add the flavoured butter and heat until it melts, then throw in the prawns and a little seasoning and stir-fry until the prawns are pink all over and cooked through, a matter of 2–3 minutes. Squeeze over some lemon juice and serve with lemon wedges.

COOK'S TIP The flavoured butter can be made in advance and kept in the fridge until needed.

ceviche

 **SmartPoints** values per serving 1
SmartPoints values per recipe 5

 **Takes 10 minutes + marinating**
Serves 6

GF

400 g very fresh sea bass or
    bream fillet, cut into chunks
1 teaspoon fine salt
1 small red onion, cubed finely
1 large red chilli, de-seeded and cubed
    finely
juice of 4–6 limes (you'll need 150 ml)
a generous handful of chopped
    fresh coriander

Fresh and zingy, ceviche is great as a tapas-style snack or served as an appetiser.

1. Place the fish in a wide, shallow bowl and coat with the salt. Set to one side for 2–3 minutes, then add the onion, chilli and lime juice, and leave to marinate for 10–15 minutes.

2. Check the seasoning, drain off any excess liquid and add the coriander. Divide into 6 portions and serve immediately.

VARIATION These flavours also work well on raw jumbo prawns (1 **SmartPoints** value) or chunks of salmon fillet (5 **SmartPoints**).

> 🍴 **COOK'S TIP** Ceviche is raw fish marinated in citrus juice. It is not cooked, but the marinating process changes the protein structure of the flesh, giving it a firmer, drier texture. Buy the freshest fish possible from a reliable source.

TOMATO AND PRAWN
courgette spaghetti

7 **SmartPoints** values per serving 7
SmartPoints values per recipe 26

Takes 25 minutes
Serves 4

2 courgettes (around 350 g), cut into
    long spaghetti-like strips (see Cook's
    tip)
150 g spaghetti
1 teaspoon olive oil
350 g shelled raw prawns
2 garlic cloves, chopped
100 ml white wine
350 g cherry tomatoes, halved
100 g Weight Watchers West Country
    thick cream (or similar)
4 tablespoons chopped fresh parsley
salt and freshly ground black pepper
lemon wedges, to serve (optional)

A delicious pasta dish that can be on the table in double-quick time – an ideal after-work meal served with a simple fresh green salad.

1. Bring a saucepan of water to the boil, add the courgette strips and simmer for 1 minute. Remove using tongs and refresh under cold water. Drain and set aside. Cook the pasta in the same water, according to the packet instructions, then drain and set aside.

2. Heat the oil in a large non-stick frying pan and add the prawns and garlic. Cook over a medium-high heat for 2–3 minutes, or until the prawns are cooked. Add the wine and bubble for 1 minute. Stir in the tomatoes and season well. Heat briefly until piping hot. Remove from the heat, stir in the cream, pasta and courgette and scatter with the parsley. Serve immediately with lemon wedges alongside, if liked.

 For a gluten free version, simply swap the spaghetti for more 'courgetti' – bringing the **SmartPoints** down to 3.

🍴 **COOK'S TIP** You can also use a spiralizer to produce a more spaghetti-like appearance, as seen in the photo opposite, top right.

PORK AND APRICOT *burgers* WITH SWEET POTATO CHIPS

 SmartPoints values per serving 14
SmartPoints values per recipe 28

Takes 30 minutes
Serves 2

1 sweet potato (300 g), cut into wedges
calorie controlled cooking spray
sea salt
125 g lean (5% fat) pork mince
35 g ready-to-eat dried apricots,
   chopped finely
2 teaspoons chopped fresh thyme
15 g toasted pine nuts, chopped
   roughly
salt and freshly ground black pepper

To serve
2 medium soft brown rolls (50 g each),
   toasted lightly
1 tablespoon 0% fat natural
   Greek yogurt
fresh salad leaves and slices of tomato

Burger and chips with a difference! And quicker than a takeaway, too.

1. Preheat the oven to Gas Mark 6/200°C/fan oven 180°C. Lay the sweet potato wedges on a large baking tray lined with non-stick baking parchment. Mist with the cooking spray, sprinkle with sea salt and roast for 30 minutes, turning once, until soft and golden.

2. Meanwhile, put the mince in a large bowl and combine with the apricots, thyme and pine nuts. Season well, then shape into 2 patties. Mist a non-stick frying or griddle pan with cooking spray and heat until hot. Cook the burgers for 8–10 minutes, turning once, until cooked through and golden. Place a burger in each of the soft rolls along with a dollop of yogurt, some salad leaves and tomato slices. Serve with the sweet potato chips on the side.

VARIATION This recipe also works well with the same amount of turkey mince or chicken mince. The **SmartPoints** values per serving will remain the same.

 For a gluten free version, use a gluten free roll instead, for a total of 15 **SmartPoints** per serving.

LEMON AND THYME
pork escalopes
WITH CHARGRILLED VEG

7 SmartPoints values per serving 7
SmartPoints value™ **SmartPoints** values per recipe 26

Takes 25 minutes
Serves 4

500 g lean pork fillet
50 g fine fresh breadcrumbs
finely grated zest of 1 lemon, plus
    lemon wedges to serve (optional)
1 tablespoon chopped fresh thyme
1 teaspoon paprika
1 egg, beaten
2 teaspoons olive oil
salt and freshly ground black pepper

For the chargrilled veg
300 g fine asparagus, trimmed
1 courgette, trimmed and sliced
    lengthways
1 red and 1 yellow pepper, de-seeded
    and sliced thickly
2 teaspoons extra virgin olive oil
a squeeze of lemon juice
2 tablespoons chopped fresh parsley

Chargrilled vegetables always look and taste great, and they go really well with these juicy pork escalopes.

1. Cut the pork fillet into 12 slices, around 1.5 cm thick, removing any visible fat. Place the slices on a chopping board, cover with greaseproof paper and lightly bash with a rolling pin to flatten slightly. Put the breadcrumbs in a bowl along with the lemon zest, thyme and paprika, and season well.

2. Dip the pork slices first in the beaten egg and then in the breadcrumb mix to lightly coat them, then set aside on a plate.

3. Meanwhile, make the chargrilled veg. Preheat the grill to its highest setting. Place all the vegetables in a shallow roasting tin, drizzle with the oil and season well. Mix thoroughly and grill for 15 minutes, or until softened and lightly charred, turning occasionally. Squeeze some lemon juice over and scatter the parsley over.

4. To cook the pork, heat half the oil in a large non-stick pan. Cook the escalopes in batches, adding the remaining oil as you need it, for around 3 minutes on each side, or until cooked through. Divide the vegetables between 4 warmed plates, with 3 pork escalopes and a wedge of lemon each, if using.

THIS RECIPE USES LOTS OF STORECUPBOARD INGREDIENTS – CHECK OUT PAGES 12–13 FOR MORE ESSENTIALS.

HAM AND PETITS POIS
pasta

SmartPoints values per serving 11
SmartPoints values per recipe 22

Takes 20 minutes
Serves 2

125 g fusilli pasta
50 g frozen petits pois
1 large egg, beaten
25 g Parmesan cheese, grated
2 slices (50 g) thick cut premium ham,
　　cut into bite-size pieces
a handful of snipped fresh chives
freshly ground black pepper

So simple, so quick, so delicious! Who needs carbonara when this pasta dish is just as tasty?

1. Cook the pasta according to the packet instructions. Just before draining, add the petits pois. Save a cup of the cooking water when you drain the pasta and petits pois.

2. Meanwhile, mix the egg with the grated Parmesan and season with black pepper.

3. Tip the drained pasta and peas back into the hot pan and stir in the egg mixture, 2 tablespoons of the reserved cooking water and the ham and chives. The residual heat should be enough to just cook the egg lightly. If not, heat it very gently for 1 minute, stirring, then serve immediately.

GF Go gluten free and use gluten free pasta instead of the fusilli – the **SmartPoints** values remain the same.

MIXED PEPPER AND
sausage pizza

SmartPoints values per serving 11
SmartPoints values per recipe 22

Takes 25 minutes
Serves 2

4 reduced fat sausages (228 g)
1 teaspoon mixed dried herbs
150 g pizza base
3 tablespoons passata with onion
    and garlic
½ x 280 g jar mixed pepper antipasto
    in balsamic vinegar, drained
    (reserve 2 tablespoons of the liquid)
½ x 125 g packet light mozzarella,
    drained and torn
mixed salad leaves, to serve
a few fresh basil leaves, to garnish
    (optional)

Using a ready-made base makes this pizza recipe simplicity itself. Ideal for a Friday night treat.

1. Preheat the oven to Gas Mark 6/200°C/fan oven 180°C. Squeeze the sausage meat from the skins into a bowl and mix together with the herbs. Shape into 12 balls and set aside.

2. Place the pizza base on a non-stick baking sheet. Spread with the passata, then top with the antipasto, mozzarella pieces and sausage balls. Bake for 12–15 minutes, or until bubbling.

3. Toss the salad leaves with the reserved liquid from the antipasto jar and serve with the pizza. Garnish with the basil, if using.

COOK'S TIP Most ready-made pizza bases come in packets of 2 – freeze 1 or double this recipe to make 2 pizzas.

BLUE CHEESE
gnocchi gratin

 SmartPoints values per serving 12
SmartPoints values per recipe 24

 Takes 30 minutes
Serves 2

calorie controlled cooking spray
a bunch of spring onions, cut into
    4 cm lengths
1 teaspoon cornflour
175 ml skimmed milk
a pinch of celery salt
50 g watercress, chopped roughly,
    plus extra to serve
250 g gnocchi
60 g dolcelatte piccante, cut into
    small chunks
freshly ground black pepper

Tangy blue cheese melts over the gnocchi to give this dish an extra creamy richness.

1. Preheat the oven to Gas Mark 6/200°C/fan oven 180°C. Mist a saucepan with the cooking spray, add the spring onions and cook for 2 minutes. Mix the cornflour with the milk until smooth, then add to the pan and cook, stirring, for 5 minutes. Add the celery salt and season with black pepper, stir in the watercress and gnocchi, then transfer the mixture to an ovenproof dish or 2 individual gratin dishes. Top with the blue cheese.

2. Bake for 10–15 minutes until bubbling. Serve immediately with the extra watercress.

ORZO *risotto* WITH WATERCRESS, BLUE CHEESE AND WALNUTS

 SmartPoints values per serving 11
SmartPoints values per recipe 44

 Takes 20 minutes
Serves 4

1 litre vegetable stock, made with
    a cube
250 g orzo pasta (see Cook's tip)
100 g watercress, chopped roughly
50 g vegetarian blue Stilton cheese,
    broken into pieces
60 g walnut pieces, toasted lightly

Orzo is a versatile rice-shaped pasta, good in soups, salads, pilaffs and risottos.

1. Pour the stock into a saucepan and bring to the boil. Add the orzo and cook until tender (it should take around 6 minutes). Drain, reserving a ladleful of the stock, and return to the pan.

2. Stir the watercress and Stilton into the orzo and add just enough stock to give it a creamy consistency. Divide between 4 bowls and scatter with the toasted walnuts. Serve immediately.

COOK'S TIP You will find orzo in larger supermarkets or Italian delicatessens. Other small flat pasta shapes, such as orecchiette, farfalline or wholewheat mafalda corta, would also work well.

NUTS ARE GREAT FOR YOU AND THE WALNUTS IN THIS RECIPE GIVE YOU A GOOD SOURCE OF PROTEIN AND HEALTHY FATS. CHECK OUT PAGES 190-1 FOR MORE ABOUT NOURISHING FOODS.

nachos WITH BLACK BEAN salsa

SmartPoints values per serving 5
SmartPoints values per recipe 32

Takes 10 minutes
Serves 6

90 g light feta cheese, crumbled
150 g cool tortilla chips

For the salsa
180 g canned black beans, drained
    and rinsed
4 spring onions, sliced
6 small vine tomatoes, chopped
6 tablespoons chopped fresh coriander
2 tablespoons lime juice, plus lime
    wedges to serve
salt and freshly ground black pepper

A Tex-Mex-inspired savoury snack that can be rustled up in moments and is perfect for sharing.

1. Combine all the ingredients for the salsa and season to taste. Serve on a platter or divide among 6 individual serving bowls. Serve with the crumbled feta and lime wedges, and arrange the tortilla chips around the edge.

> **COOK'S TIP** Black beans are widely used in South American cuisine. They are small and creamy – perfect for salsa. If you can't find them, use the same amount of black eyed beans instead. The **SmartPoints** values will stay the same.

TOP 10 foods TO NOURISH YOU

You'll find all of these great foods in the recipes in this book.

2 KALE

If you're looking for kale you'll probably stumble across the 'curly' variety in your local supermarket. A 60 g serving provides one and a half times your recommended intake of vitamin C. It also contains iron and vitamin A, making kale a great germ-busting, skin-, hair- and nail-enhancing ingredient to add to a recipe. It's a great addition to many dishes but be careful not to overcook it as it can end up tasting bitter.

3 BROCCOLI

This is a 'super green'. Not only does it contain iron, it's also a source of non-dairy calcium (perfect if you can't have dairy). It contains vitamins A and C needed for healthy eyes and immune system. It cooks in minutes and is really versatile. Throw it into a stir-fry, add it to your salad, or serve it with your favourite Sunday roast.

1 BEETROOT

This humble vegetable has been around forever and is known to help reduce blood pressure. It is also full of fibre, keeping the digestive system functioning well, and can help to keep the liver functioning properly. Try it in a soup – it's delicious – or roast it and add to your salad. Check out our Warm beet, baby kale and halloumi salad on page 198.

4 BLUEBERRIES

These little berries are bursting with antioxidants, which help to fight cancer-causing free radicals. They also contain vitamin C to help keep the immune system working and fibre for aiding digestion and helping to keep your heart healthy. We have a Blueberry soy smoothie recipe on page 132 – it's tasty and will also increase your intake of these fabulous berries.

5 SOCCA

Bread made using gluten free gram (chickpea) flour is perfect for people who follow a gluten free diet. It is high in protein and low in sugar. If making a loaf seems a bit daunting right now then check out our recipe on page 196 for our socca pancakes – yum!

6 GARLIC

We use this mainly for flavour; however, the health benefits of garlic are massive. It can help to reduce blood pressure and cholesterol, and this can have a positive impact on heart health.

7 PUMPKIN SEEDS

These contain zinc, which is essential for maintaining a healthy immune system and also works to release serotonin, which affects mood and promotes sleep. You can eat pumpkin seeds raw or lightly toasted. Liven up any salad or soup by sprinkling these tasty seeds on top. See page 150 for our Butternut squash and coriander soup recipe.

8 NUTS

Nuts are a great source of protein and healthy fats, which the body needs to grow and repair and to carry out certain functions. We're not just talking dry roasted or salted; there are lots of different types of nuts for you to choose from – just check out the wholefoods section of your local supermarket. For an alternative to peanut butter, you'll find our Nutty butters on page 204.

9 CHIA SEEDS

High in protein and fibre, chia seeds are a great weight-loss aid as they will keep you fuller for longer. They are also a good non-dairy source of calcium, and you can add them to salads, yogurt, cereal, or bake them into bars. Store them in the fridge to keep them fresh. Try our Chia seed snack bar recipe on page 212.

10 FREEKEH

This is a protein-packed grain that is becoming more and more popular. It keeps you fuller for longer and is high in fibre, which is great for your digestive health. Look out for it on your next shop! Check out page 200 for our Orange freekeh chicken recipe.

STAY HYDRATED: IT HELPS ENERGY AND CONCENTRATION LEVELS AND WATER IS NEEDED BY EVERY CELL IN THE BODY. HAVE AROUND 2 LITRES OF FLUID EACH DAY. IF YOU'RE INCREASING ACTIVITY LEVELS YOU'LL NEED MORE.

superclean

BEETROOT QUINOA *risotto* WITH GOAT'S CHEESE

SmartPoints values per serving 11
SmartPoints values per recipe 22

Takes 45–60 minutes
Serves 2

2 large beetroot, trimmed, scrubbed
      and chopped into bite-size pieces
120 g quinoa, rinsed in cold water
2 teaspoons olive oil
1 large onion, chopped finely
2 celery sticks, chopped finely
500 ml vegetable stock (see page 220)
1 bay leaf
60 g soft goat's cheese, crumbled
1 tablespoon snipped fresh chives
salt and freshly ground black pepper

Quinoa is a good source of protein and can be used in many dishes in place of bulgur wheat, couscous and rice.

1. Preheat the oven to Gas Mark 6/200°C/fan oven 180°C. Wrap the beetroot in foil and roast for 45–60 minutes until tender. Set aside.

2. While the beetroot is cooking, heat the quinoa in a large saucepan for a few minutes to drive off any water, then add the oil, onion and celery. Continue cooking over a low heat for around 10 minutes until the onion and celery have softened, stirring frequently to prevent them catching and adding a little water if they do.

3. Add the stock and bay leaf, and simmer gently for around 10–12 minutes, stirring occasionally, until the liquid is almost all absorbed and the quinoa is tender.

4. Stir in the beetroot, season to taste and serve with the goat's cheese sprinkled over and scattered with the chives.

> **COOK'S TIP** If you need to save time with this dish, buy ready-cooked beetroot. Chop and warm through with the quinoa before serving.

socca WITH ROASTED PEPPERS, TOMATOES AND AVOCADO

8 SmartPoints values per serving 8
SmartPoints values per recipe 32

Takes 35 minutes
Serves 4

2 orange or red peppers, halved,
  de-seeded and chopped roughly
300 g cherry tomatoes, halved
3 teaspoons olive oil
1 teaspoon fresh thyme leaves
2 red onions, peeled and sliced thinly
a pinch of dried chilli flakes
1 avocado, halved, stoned and chopped
lime wedges, to serve

For the pancakes
150 g chickpea flour (gram flour)
1 teaspoon dried thyme
2 teaspoons olive oil
1 egg white
salt and freshly ground black pepper

These pancakes are made from chickpea (gram) flour which is gluten free and packed with protein.

1. Preheat the oven to Gas Mark 6/200°C/fan oven 180°C. Combine the peppers, tomatoes, half the olive oil and thyme leaves in a roasting tin and cook for 20 minutes until softened and beginning to char.

2. In the meantime, heat the remaining oil in heavy based pan, add the onions, stir to coat and leave on a low heat, stirring occasionally until light brown and really soft. This will take around 20 minutes. Stir in the chilli flakes.

3. To make the pancakes, stir together the flour and thyme with some salt and pepper. Whisk the oil with 250 ml water, make a well in the flour and gradually beat in the liquid. Whisk the egg white to form soft peaks and fold into the batter. Heat a non-stick frying pan until hot, add a ladleful of batter and cook for a minute or so until you see bubbles on the surface, then carefully loosen and flip over to cook for another minute. Keep warm in the oven while cooking the rest of the pancakes.

4. Serve 2 pancakes each, spread with some of the caramelised onions, topped with the roasted veg and some avocado, and with a lime wedge on the side.

> **🍴 COOK'S TIP** These pancakes make a great base for pizza toppings or can be cooked for a further 5–10 minutes in a medium oven to crisp up more like flatbreads.

SOCCA IS A GREAT GLUTEN FREE BREAD – FIND OUT MORE ABOUT IT ON PAGE 191.

WARM BEETROOT, BABY KALE AND
halloumi salad

SmartPoints values per serving 11
SmartPoints values per recipe 22

 Takes 45–60 minutes
Serves 2

2 medium beetroot, trimmed, scrubbed
    and chopped roughly into even-
    sized pieces
25 g walnut pieces
60 g baby kale
60 g Little Gem lettuce, torn or
    chopped roughly
2 teaspoons olive oil
1 teaspoon cider vinegar
110 g light halloumi cheese, sliced
salt and freshly ground black pepper

The sweetness of roasted beetroot is lovely with the tang of salty halloumi in this warm salad. Baby kale has a light peppery taste and is available in some supermarkets.

1. Preheat the oven to Gas Mark 6/200°C/fan oven 180°C. Wrap the beetroot pieces in foil and roast for 45–60 minutes until tender.

2. Meanwhile, dry-fry the walnuts for 1–2 minutes until you can just smell their aroma. Set aside.

3. Divide the baby kale and lettuce between 2 plates. Combine the olive oil and cider vinegar with a little salt and pepper.

4. Heat a griddle or frying pan and cook the halloumi for about 1 minute, turning once, until just golden.

5. Scatter the beetroot over the leaves, followed by the halloumi and nuts. Serve drizzled with the dressing.

COOK'S TIP If you feel the need for some carbs, toss in 60 g dry quinoa, cooked according to the packet instructions, drained and seasoned, for an extra 3 **SmartPoints** values per serving.

Roasted beetroot will keep wrapped in the fridge for 4–5 days and is great added to salads or served as a side vegetable with meat.

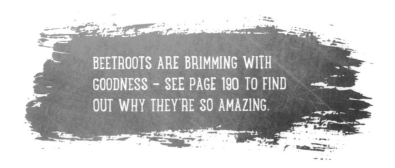

BEETROOTS ARE BRIMMING WITH GOODNESS – SEE PAGE 190 TO FIND OUT WHY THEY'RE SO AMAZING.

ORANGE FREEKEH *chicken*

5 SmartPoints values per serving 5
SmartPoints values per recipe 18

Preparation time 15 minutes
Cooking time 30–35 minutes
Serves 4

50 g freekeh (or freekeh and
    quinoa mixed)
3 teaspoons olive oil
1 onion, chopped finely
1 clove garlic, chopped
40 g pitted Kalamata olives in brine,
    chopped
1 tablespoon fresh parsley, chopped
1 orange, segmented (retain any juice)
4 x 150 g skinless chicken breasts
300 ml vegetable stock (see page 220)
salt and freshly ground black pepper

Freekeh is a green wheat that is toasted, giving it a mild smoky flavour. High in protein and fibre, it cooks quickly and can be used in salads or as an alternative to rice.

1. Bring a saucepan of water to the boil, add the freekeh or freekeh mix and cook for 12–15 minutes until tender. Drain.

2. Heat 1 teaspoon of the the oil in frying pan large enough to hold all 4 chicken breasts, add the onion and cook for 10 minutes until softened. Add the garlic and cook for a further minute. Stir the onion mixture into the freekeh with the olives and parsley. Finely grate the zest from the orange and mix in with some salt and pepper.

3. Flatten the chicken breasts between two sheets of parchment using a rolling pin. Spread some of the freekeh stuffing over each, then roll up and pin with a wooden cocktail stick. (You may not use it all.)

4. Heat the remaining oil in the frying pan, add the chicken breasts and cook, turning to brown all over, for around 5 minutes. Add the stock, cover and simmer for 10–15 minutes until cooked through. Add the orange segments and juice and stir any extra filling into the sauce for the final minute to heat through.

GO TO PAGES 190-1 TO FIND OUT
MORE ABOUT FREEKEH AND OTHER
GOOD-FOR-YOU FOODS.

ZESTY *trout* WITH WARM BROAD AND BUTTER BEANS

SmartPoints values per serving 8
SmartPoints values per recipe 16

 Takes 20 minutes
Serves 2

10 g whole almonds, cut in slivers
130 g frozen broad beans, defrosted
  (100 g podded weight, if using
  fresh)
120 g canned butter beans (drained
  weight)
3 teaspoons olive oil
zest and juice of 1 lemon
2 x 100 g trout fillets
2 handfuls of watercress, chopped
  roughly
1 tablespoon snipped fresh chives
salt and freshly ground black pepper
lemon wedges, to serve

Fresh and summery, broad beans have a fantastic bright green colour when popped from their greyish skins.

1. Dry-fry the almonds in a small pan until golden, moving them around the pan so that they don't catch. Remove from the pan and set aside.

2. Slip the broad beans from their grey skins and place them in the pan with the drained butter beans. Combine 2 teaspoons of the olive oil with the lemon zest and juice and add to the pan.

3. Heat a non-stick frying pan with the remaining oil. Season the trout on both sides and fry the fish for around 2 minutes on each side until the flesh just flakes.

4. While the trout is cooking, warm the beans through then remove from the heat and stir in the watercress and chives. Serve the trout on a bed of beans and scattered with the almonds, and with a lemon wedge for squeezing.

nutty butters

SmartPoints values per serving 2
SmartPoints values per recipe 37

 GF

 **V**

Takes 10–15 minutes
**Makes 20 teaspoons (1 teaspoon =
      1 serving)**

200 g whole almonds (i.e. not
      blanched)
1 teaspoon honey
sea salt, to taste

These are so easy to make and taste delicious – simply grind the nuts until you have a coarse paste and you are ready to tuck in! Use to spread on rice crackers, wholemeal or rye bread, and to stir into natural yogurts.

1. Preheat the oven to Gas Mark 4/180°C/fan oven 160°C. Spread the nuts out on a baking tray and roast for 5–10 minutes until you can just smell them and they have turned a slightly darker shade.

2. Place in a food processor and blend. It will take some time to crush the nuts enough to release the oils, so don't think it isn't working. Stop every now and then and scrape down the sides before continuing. Once you have a paste, add the honey, taste and add a pinch of salt to your taste. Store, covered, in the fridge for up to a month.

HAZELNUT AND CACAO

SmartPoints values per serving 2 **SmartPoints** values per recipe 43
Follow the recipe above using **hazelnuts** (see Cook's tip) instead of almonds and adding **15 g cacao powder** once you have created a paste. Add the honey and taste, adding salt if you like.

ALMOND AND ORANGE

SmartPoints values per serving 2 **SmartPoints** values per recipe 37
Follow the basic nut recipe, adding **1 teaspoon finely grated orange zest** at the end.

PECAN AND MAPLE

SmartPoints values per serving 2 **SmartPoints** values per recipe 46
Make the nut butter using **pecans** instead of almonds and stir in **2 teaspoons maple syrup** in place of the honey.

> **¶ COOK'S TIP** Roasting the nuts beforehand adds to the depth of flavour and helps to drive off any moisture. Use any nut you like, preferably unblanched, and definitely unsalted. If using hazelnuts, roast and then rub your hands over them to discard the papery skins before processing.

NUTS ARE SO GOOD FOR YOU – FIND OUT MORE ABOUT THEM AND SOME OTHER GREAT FOODS ON PAGES 190–1.

original

almond and orange

pecan and maple

hazelnut and cacao

SUMMER BERRY *spread*

 SmartPoints values per serving 1
SmartPoints values per recipe 9

 Takes 10 minutes
Makes 160 g (1 teaspoon = 1 serving)

200 g mixed berries, fresh or frozen
3 tablespoons maple syrup

This is a fresh fruity spread you can use in the same way as jam – to flavour yogurts, spread on crackers or stir into a rice pudding. Delicious!

1. Place the berries in a small pan and heat gently to release the juices. Roughly mash to further release the juices, then stir in the maple syrup and simmer, stirring occasionally, for 5 minutes until it is thick enough to drag a spoon through and leave the base of the pan visible.

2. Cool and cover before storing in the fridge for up to 1 week.

TROPICAL
fruit salad

 SmartPoints values per serving 0
SmartPoints values per recipe 0

 **Takes 10 minutes + chilling**
Serves 2

1 ripe papaya, peeled and halved
¼ pineapple, peeled, cored and
    chopped
½ ripe mango, peeled and chopped
zest and juice of 1 lime
1 passion fruit

An exotic fruit medley that will make the perfect end to any meal.

1. Scoop out the black seeds from the papaya and chop the flesh. Mix with the pineapple and mango in a bowl and squeeze over the lime juice.

2. Add the seeds and pulp from the passion fruit and divide the mixture between 2 bowls. Cover and chill in the fridge until ready to serve, decorated with lime zest.

> **COOK'S TIP** Look out for papaya with yellow skin, as these are the ripest.

buckwheat PANCAKES
WITH COCONUT YOGURT

SmartPoints values per serving 8
SmartPoints values per recipe 31

Takes 30 minutes + resting
Serves 4

120 g buckwheat flour
1 egg
200 ml skimmed milk
1 teaspoon vegetable oil
15 g unsweetened desiccated coconut
170 g 0% fat natural Greek yogurt
4 teaspoons runny honey
½ teaspoon vanilla extract
300 g fresh pineapple, cut in thin slices

Buckwheat is a gluten free grain-like seed that has a lovely nutty flavour. It works well in pancakes, bread and cakes.

1. To make the batter, place the flour, egg, milk and oil into a food processor and blend until smooth. Alternatively, gradually beat the wet ingredients into the flour in a large mixing bowl. Set the batter aside to rest for 10 minutes.

2. Dry-fry the coconut in a small non-stick frying pan, moving it around the pan for a couple of minutes until it is golden. Stir three-quarters of it into the yogurt with 2 teaspoons of the honey and the vanilla extract.

3. Reheat the frying pan, add a ladleful of batter and swirl round the pan. Cook for 1 minute until the underside is golden, then flip and cook for another minute before sliding on to a plate and covering to keep warm. Repeat to make 8 pancakes.

4. Once the pancakes are all cooked, pan-fry the pineapple slices until charred. Serve 2 pancakes each with the pineapple and yogurt, drizzled with the rest of the honey and scattered with the remaining coconut.

> **COOK'S TIP** If gluten free is essential to your diet, check the flour packets as some brands are ground in the same mill as wheat and may contain gluten for that reason.
>
> You don't have to pan-fry the pineapple but the caramelisation adds to the natural sweetness of the dish.

chia seed
SNACK BARS

 8 SmartPoints values per serving 8
SmartPoints values per recipe 77

 GF **Preparation time 15 minutes**
Cooking time 25–30 minutes
+ cooling
 V **Makes 10**

2 tablespoons chia seeds
100 g stoned dates, chopped roughly
25 ml coconut oil
50 g sultanas
50 g dried ready-to-eat apricots, chopped
40 g pumpkin seeds
finely grated zest of 1 orange
200 g porridge oats

These are refined-sugar free, vegan and packed with cleanness! They will give you a slow energy release so make a great breakfast or snack.

1. Preheat the oven to Gas Mark 3/160°C/fan oven 140°C. Line a 26 x 16 cm tin with baking parchment. Soak the chia seeds in a small bowl with 120 ml cold water for around 5 minutes, or until they swell and thicken.

2. Place the dates and coconut oil in a medium pan with 2 tablespoons water on a low heat. Stir continuously for a few minutes until the coconut oil has melted and the mixture becomes a thick paste – it doesn't have to be completely smooth. Remove from the heat and blend in 100 ml cold water.

3. Add the remaining ingredients to the pan with the soaked chia seeds and mix well. Spoon into the tin and level the surface, pressing the mixture into the corners. Bake for 25–30 minutes until dark brown. Remove from the oven and cool in the tin for 10 minutes before cutting into 10 bars. Store in an airtight container for 3–4 days.

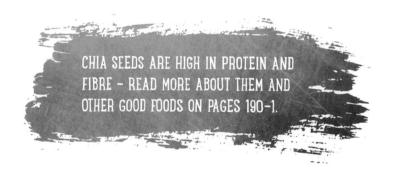

CHIA SEEDS ARE HIGH IN PROTEIN AND FIBRE – READ MORE ABOUT THEM AND OTHER GOOD FOODS ON PAGES 190-1.

RAW brownies

SmartPoints values per serving 7
SmartPoints values per recipe 65

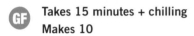

Takes 15 minutes + chilling
Makes 10

200 g dried dates, chopped roughly
75 g whole almonds
75 g walnuts
40 g cacao

These no-cook brownies are unbelievably easy to make and are full of valuable nutrients.

1. Line a 10 x 18 cm freezerproof dish with cling film or parchment. Place the dates in a small bowl and cover with warm water. Set aside to soak for 5 minutes.

2. Place the nuts in a food processor and grind until fine and crumb-like – don't over-blend or you'll have nut butter! Add the cacao and blend to combine. Remove from the processor to a bowl.

3. Drain the dates, add to the processor and blend until coarsely sticky. Add the nut mixture back in and blend to combine. Press into the dish and then freeze for 10 minutes before tipping out and cutting into 10 pieces. Store in the fridge for a couple of days, or freeze until required.

romesco

SmartPoints values per serving 3
SmartPoints values per recipe 10

Takes 35 minutes
Makes 345 g (136 g = 1 serving)

2 red peppers, halved and de-seeded
150 g tomatoes
6 garlic cloves
25 g whole almonds
½ teaspoon white wine vinegar
1 tablespoon olive oil
salt and freshly ground black pepper

This sauce is great stirred into pasta, or served alongside roast chicken, hot or cold. It can be frozen for up to 1 month.

1. Preheat the oven to Gas Mark 6/200°C/fan oven 180°C. Place the peppers, tomatoes and whole garlic cloves in a roasting tin. Cook for 20 minutes until the skin of the peppers begins to char. Roast the nuts alongside the peppers for the final 5 minutes, until slightly darker.

2. Once cooked, place the peppers in a plastic bag, seal and leave to steam for 10 minutes.

3. Grind the nuts in a food processor or blender. Skin the tomatoes and peppers and add to the processor or blender. Squeeze the soft garlic from its skin and add to the processor with the vinegar and oil, scraping out any juices from the roasting tin. Blend to a rough sauce, season and store in an airtight container for up to 1 week.

harissa

SmartPoints values per serving 1
SmartPoints values per recipe 5

Takes 15–20 minutes
Serves 4 (56 g = 1 serving)

1 red pepper, halved and de-seeded
½ teaspoon cumin seeds
1 teaspoon coriander seeds
3 garlic cloves, peeled and chopped
3 red chillies, halved, de-seeded
    and chopped
5 fresh mint leaves
1 tablespoon olive oil

A spicy, garlicky paste that is lovely stirred into freekeh or quinoa or used to marinate chicken or lamb.

1. Preheat the grill to high and toast the pepper until the skin blisters. Place in a plastic bag and leave to steam for 10 minutes.

2. Dry-fry the seeds for a minute or so until you can just smell them.

3. Peel the skin from the pepper and chop roughly. Place in a mini blender with the seeds, garlic and chillies. Blend to a coarse paste then add the mint and oil and blitz to combine. Store, covered, in the fridge for up to 1 week.

romesco

harissa

TOMATO
ketchup

SmartPoints values per serving 1
SmartPoints values per recipe 5

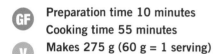
Preparation time 10 minutes
Cooking time 55 minutes
Makes 275 g (60 g = 1 serving)

1 shallot, peeled and sliced
1 garlic clove, peeled and chopped
450 g tomatoes, chopped roughly
100 ml white wine vinegar
25 g stoned dates, chopped
1 teaspoon peppercorns
1 bay leaf
1 star anise

Although this takes time to cook the preparation is easy. Commercial tomato ketchup contains refined sugar and preservatives so it's well worth making a batch of this tangy 'clean-living' sauce.

1. Place all the ingredients in a heavy based pan, bring to the boil, then reduce the heat and simmer gently for 45 minutes. Remove the bay leaf and star anise, then use a hand-held blender to blend the sauce until smooth.

2. Sieve the sauce to remove any bits, then return to a clean pan and boil until thickened, around 10 minutes. Cover and store in the fridge for up to 2 weeks.

YOU HAVE TO JUST LOVE TOMATOES FOR THEIR VERSATILITY! CHECK OUT PAGES 12–13 FOR MORE STORECUPBOARD ESSENTIALS.

VEGETABLE
stock

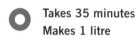

SmartPoints values per serving 0
SmartPoints values per recipe 0

Takes 35 minutes
Makes 1 litre

1 large onion
3 celery sticks
1 large carrot
2 bay leaves
2 sprigs of fresh thyme
1 sprig of fresh rosemary
5 peppercorns
1 litre boiling water

The longer you simmer this, the better the flavour, but it can be done in 30 minutes if you don't have time to spare. Season with salt and freshly ground black pepper when adding it to your recipe, then you can balance the flavour of any other ingredients.

1. Peel, wash and roughly chop the vegetables and place in a large saucepan. Add the herbs and peppercorns. Pour over the water, bring up to the boil, cover and simmer for 30 minutes. Strain.

> **COOK'S TIP** You can use the strained vegetables in soup, or chop and stir into pasta. The stock can be kept in the fridge for a few days or can be frozen.

Index